DASH DIET COOKBOOK

21-DAY MEDITERRANEAN DASH DIET MEAL PLAN TO IMPROVE YOUR HEALTH AND LOSE WEIGHT WITH EASY AND QUICK RECIPES. WITH MORE THAN 125 DELECTABLE RECIPES!

By

Marla Smith

TABLE OF CONTENTS

INTRODUCTION	2
CHAPTER 1: WHAT IS THE DASH DIET?	3
CHAPTER 2: BENEFITS OF THE DASH DIET	9
CHAPTER 3: IMPORTANCE OF HEALTHY WEIGHT	13
CHAPTER 4: HEALTH BENEFITS OF CONSUMING GOOD FATS	17
CHAPTER 5: ENHANCE YOUR RESULTS WITH EXERCISE	24
CHAPTER 6: BREAKFAST RECIPES	33
CHAPTER 7: LUNCH RECIPES	71
CHAPTER 8: DINNER RECIPES	110
CHAPTER 9: SIDE DISH RECIPES	145
CHAPTER 10: DESSERT RECIPES	180
CONCLUSION	213

Introduction

The DASH diet is an ideal way to quickly bring down your blood pressure through correcting bad eating habits. Even though the approach shows a much healthier eating plan it's still important not to overeat. If you're planning on following the DASH for weight loss then you can be a little more flexible with your foods but you'll want to be stricter with your calories.

Within 2 Weeks you should see an improvement in your blood pressure numbers and potentially some weight loss. Make sure you're keeping hydrated to flush out excess sodium.

Potassium, Magnesium, Calcium, and Whole grains are all important in the DASH approach so try and find foods that are rich in these nutrients. Stay away from added sugar and salt as much as possible.

The reason the DASH approach is so successful in such a short time is that it's making sure your body has the nutrients it needs and avoiding the products that aggravate the problem. Don't forget to plan ahead for times when you might consider snacking.

Remember, the DASH approach isn't about denying you any of the foods you want, simply making healthier choices or versions of them. If you happen to have a day where you haven't been strict don't worry about it. A cheat day does everyone good, just try not to make it too often.

Exercise and a healthy lifestyle are also part of the DASH approach, if you're tweaking your diet why not tweak other things too that can really make a big impact on your numbers.

Even if you don't stick to the meal plans hopefully you've gotten enough information to learn more about the DASH diet and what you should be doing to form your own. With all this information you're sure to see a quick improvement in your numbers.

Chapter 1: What is the DASH Diet?

I'm sure you've been through diets in your life. If not you, you must have known people who begin a diet enthusiastically, then hit a plateau and give it all up in frustration and resume their unhealthy eating habits. Wondering what the DASH diet is all about? It's a one of a kind diet, specifically designed to reduce blood pressure levels in people. Hypertension, or high blood pressure, is one of the greatest silent killers of this century.

The DASH diet is rich in fruits, vegetables, whole grains, and low-fat dairy products. Its emphasis isn't on deprivation, but on adaptation. The DASH diet aims to change the way people look at food, to educate them about their bodies, and to teach them to make healthy, sustainable choices.

The DASH diet was created to change lives by changing lifestyles. Unlike more restrictive diets, the DASH diet was designed to be approachable, and to be readily incorporated into people's lives. For the most part, you do not need to shop at special grocery stores or go through agonizing transition periods; you just need to start adjusting your food patterns, one step at a time.

The basics of the DASH diet are simple: Eat more fruits, vegetables, whole grains, and lean protein, and eat less saturated fat, salt, and sweets. It's a common-sense approach to health that really works.

Why the DASH Diet Works

The DASH diet works because it's a lifestyle that can be sustained easily, not a traditional diet. The word "diet" conjures thoughts of temporary deprivation, but the DASH diet is the opposite. It aims at educating individuals on how they can undertake clean or proper eating, on a daily basis, so that they build healthy bodies. Rather than impose strict controls on food content, such as the total number of fats, DASH diet follows important rules of choosing clean foods. When individuals understand the implications of their daily dietary decision making, they're much more likely to choose wisely. Therefore, it is easy to adopt the DASH diet.

The ultimate goal of the DASH diet is to reduce the intake of harmful foods and to choose healthy substitutes instead. When you understand the damage that bad food does to your body, it makes you far less interested in eating it. And once you wean yourself from excess fat, cholesterol, sodium, and sugar, you will be amazed by how much better you feel! Bad food takes its toll in so many ways, not just silently with hypertension and heart disease, but also outwardly in your appearance, energy level, and enthusiasm for life. If you are feeling sluggish, consider what you last ate. Was it good for you? Or bad? Unless you are fueling your body with good food, it will fail you. The DASH diet isn't a strict dietary regimen, but rather a new way of seeing, appreciating, and consuming food.

Grains, vegetables, fruits, low-fat dairy products, seeds, nuts, and lean meat all form the base of the DASH diet. So, there are no strict restrictions, only amazing benefits. Besides giving you a way of turning to healthy eating habits, the DASH diet is primarily known for showing great results in lowering high blood pressure. This diet is rich in several minerals like calcium, zinc, iron, manganese, and potassium, and these nutrients primarily help to regulate the blood pressure. Also, the diet is low in saturated fat and cholesterol but provides a significant amount of protein, which can also help people suffering from high blood pressure.

Knowing what kind of foods make the foundation of this diet makes it clear that it can also be used to lose weight and excess fat. Following this kind of diet means losing about 500 calories a day. Combine that with exercise, and you will get slim fast. What supports this is also the fact that the DASH diet, rich in protein and fiber, keeps you satiated for longer periods and thus prevents overeating and gaining weight.

The DASH diet is one of the few diets that can help you meet your daily requirement for potassium, which, besides countering the effect of salt to raise blood pressure, also helps in preventing osteoporosis. This diet also provides sufficient amounts of vitamin B 12, calcium, and fiber, which are required for proper cell metabolism, building and maintaining strong bones, keeping blood sugar levels stable, and preventing obesity.

DASH Diet Health Plan

Dash diet for high blood pressure/hypertension

Your daily sodium intake from food should be between 1500 and 2300 milligrams per day. The latter is the highest level of sodium that is acceptable according to the National High Blood Pressure Education

Program. This is also the amount that is recommended by the US Dietary Guidelines for Americans. 1500 Milligrams is the ideal amount of sodium per day according to the Institute of Medicine. This is the level that you should eventually strive for.

Blood pressure will gradually reduce as you reduce the amount of sodium you consume. DASH menus usually contain 2300 milligrams of sodium to help lower blood pressure gradually. On average, most men consume close to 4200 milligrams of sodium and women consume 3300 milligrams of sodium per day – which is significantly higher than the suggested levels.

The DASH diet consists of food that is low in sodium suitable for patients suffering from blood pressure. With DASH diet, you will experience multiple benefits that you can help you stabilize your blood pressure levels. When you follow a combination of a balanced eating plan and also work towards reducing the sodium content in food, you will be able to prevent the development of high blood pressure.

Dash diet for weight loss

Dash Diet indeed helps to trim your weight by various indirect means.

While the DASH diet does not focus on reducing calories, it fills up your diet with very nutrient dense foods as opposed to ones that are rich in calories, this helps to shed off a few pounds!

This diet is a great way to lose weight because it incorporates fresh, whole foods and reduces packaged, processed foods that are filled with empty calories. Not only will you lose weight, you'll also have a better chance of keeping it off. DASH goes beyond the calorie counting and helps you establish sound eating habits that improve your chances for maintaining healthy weight.

Being on a diet full of veggies and fruits, you will consume lots of fiber, which is also believed to help in weight loss.

Apart from that, the diet also controls your appetite since cleaner and nutrition dense foods will keep you satisfied throughout the whole day. Lowering the food intake will further contribute to weight loss.

Steps towards Transitioning to the DASH Diet

Changing your eating habits needs to be done gradually. Here are a few suggestions to help you make an easy transition to the DASH diet:

Keep a journal and track your eating habits. What do you eat for breakfast, lunch, and dinner? How often do you eat in between meals, and what are you snacking on? From your journal, you can figure out where you need to make changes. For example, add a cup or two of vegetables and fruits to help reduce too many servings of meat. Limit your sodium and sugar by reading the nutrition facts labels on food packages.

When shopping, choose "low-fat," "non-fat," "no sugar added," "no cholesterol," and other healthier versions of products. For grain servings, choose whole grains, such as whole wheat bread and whole grain cereals.

If you love butter or margarine, decrease the amount you use by half and switch to no-cholesterol and low-sodium versions. You can use spices as a substitute for salt. Experiment with different herbs if you're not sure how they taste. Some examples of spices you can try are rosemary, basil, nutmeg, parsley, sage, and thyme.

Chapter 2:   Benefits of the DASH Diet

Now that we have discussed what the DASH Diet is and since you have an overview already lets go to its health benefits. The DASH diet comes with a range of health benefits. Following are some of the major advantages of following the DASH diet:

Cardiovascular Health

The DASH diet decreases your consumption of refined carbohydrates by increasing your consumption of foods high in potassium and dietary fiber (fruits, vegetables, and whole grains). In addition, it diminishes your consumption of saturated fats. Therefore, the DASH diet has a favorable effect on your lipid profile and glucose tolerance, which reduces the prevalence of metabolic syndrome (MS) in post-menopausal women.

Reports state that a diet limited to 500 calories favors a loss of 17% of total body weight in 6 months in overweight women. This reduces the prevalence of MS by 15%. However, when this diet follows the patterns of the DASH diet, while triglycerides decrease in a similar way, the reduction in weight and BP is even greater.

It also reduces blood sugar and increases HDL, which decreases the prevalence of MS in 35% of women. These results contrast with those of other studies, which have reported that the DASH diet alone, i.e., without caloric restriction, does not affect HDL and glycemia. This means that the effects of the DASH diet on MS are associated mainly with the greater reduction in BP and that, for more changes, the diet would be required to be combined with weight loss.

Helpful for Patients with Diabetes

The DASH diet has also been shown to help reduce inflammatory and coagulation factors (C-reactive protein and fibrinogen) in patients with diabetes. These benefits are associated with the contribution of antioxidants and fibers, given the high consumption of fruits and vegetables that the DASH diet requires. In addition, the DASH diet has been shown to reduce total cholesterol and LDL, which reduces the estimated 10-year cardiovascular risk. Epidemiological studies have determined that women in the highest quintile of food consumption according to the DASH diet have a 24% to 33% lower risk of coronary events and an 18% lower risk of a cerebrovascular event. Similarly, a meta-analysis of six observational studies has determined that the DASH diet can reduce the risk of cardiovascular events by 20%.

Weight Reduction

Limited research associates the DASH diet, in isolation, with weight reduction. In some studies, weight reduction was greater when the subject was on the DASH diet as compared to an isocaloric controlled diet. This could be related to the higher calcium intake and lower energy density of the DASH diet. The American guidelines for the treatment of obesity emphasize that, regardless of diet, a caloric restriction would be the most important factor in reducing weight.

However, several studies have made an association between (1) greater weight and fat loss in diets and (2) caloric restriction and higher calcium intake. Studies have also observed an inverse association between dairy consumption and body mass index (BMI). In obese patients, weight loss has been reported as being 170% higher after 24 weeks on a hypocaloric diet with high calcium intake.

In addition, the loss of trunk fat was reported to be 34% of the total weight loss as compared to only 21% in a control diet. It has also been determined that a calcium intake of 20 mg per gram has a protective effect in overweight middle-aged women. This would be equivalent to 1275 mg of calcium for a western diet of 1700 kcal. It has been suggested that low calcium intake increases the circulating level of the parathyroid hormone and vitamin D, which have been shown to increase the level of cytosolic calcium in adipocytes in vitro, changing the metabolism of lipolysis to lipogenesis.

Despite these reports, the effect that diet-provided calcium has on women's weight after menopause is a controversial subject. An epidemiological study has noted that a sedentary lifestyle and, to a lesser extent, caloric intake are associated with post- menopausal weight gain, though calcium intake is not associated with it. The average calcium intake in this group of women is approximately 1000 mg, which would be low, as previously stated. Another study of post-menopausal women shows that calcium and vitamin D supplementation in those with a calcium intake of less than 1200 mg per day decreases the risk of weight gain by 11%.

In short, the DASH diet is favorable, both in weight control and in the regulation of fatty tissue deposits, due to its high calcium content (1200 mg/day). The contribution of calcium apparently plays a vital role in the regulation of lipogenesis.

Now that we have established the myriad benefits of the DASH diet, let's check out some of the most delicious and unique DASH diet recipes for all times of the day!

Chapter 3: Importance of Healthy Weight

When we think of losing our excess weight, we often wonder what goal to set. But it is ideal to set 6 pounds as the weight loss goal and you have to lose it in 10 weeks. Here are some tips to bear in mind when you wish to do so.

- The very first tip is to eat a bowl of vegetables with each and every meal. Pick the best and freshest ones and don't season it with any salt or pepper. You can try a different color vegetable and steam it. If it is a soft vegetable then try to have it raw. You will see that your body is getting healthier with each meal and your palette will get used to eating vegetables on a regular basis.

- You must consume half a cup or bowl of nuts and seeds on a daily basis. You can have it twice if your palette allows it or stick to just one cup per day. You must not consume the salted variety and can prepare it at home with ease. Place 1 cup almond, 1-cup cashews and 1 cup unsalted pistachios in a pan and dry roast it. Allow it to cool down and place in an airtight container. You must eat at least half cup of this on a regular basis.

- You should limit your consumption of fatty meats. You have to remove the skin from your meats in order to make them diet friendly. You should also avoid the meats that are slightly salty like fish. You should clean the meats externally and cook it well in order to get rid of the sodium content. If you wish to use broth to cook it then you should use only homemade broth that is free from sodium.

- You should avoid dairy and soya product at least for the first 4 weeks of the diet. These have the tendency of increasing your body's fat content. If you are too used to these then you can replace them with nut extracts such as nut milk and nut yogurt. But you should limit these as well and have them in measured quantities.

- You have to cut out junk and processed foods from your diet at all costs. They have the tendency of filling up your body with all unnecessary chemicals that can make you extremely unhealthy. Try to come up with healthier versions of the diet.

- You have to drink at least 10 to 12 glasses of water a day. You can fill up a few bottles and label them. As soon as you finish the first bottle move to the next and then to the next etc.

- You have to exercise at least 40 minutes a day. The first 20 minutes should be hardcore cardio and the rest can be weights or floor exercises. You have to keep it as diverse as possible. Try to exercise at least 4 days a week.

- You might have to consume a few supplements that are laden with vitamins and minerals when you are following such a diet and exercise regime. You should consult a dietician for it and he or she might give you the appropriate advice.

These form the different things that you should do when you wish to lose this type of weight in 10 weeks. You have to buy yourself a quality weighing scale and weigh yourself from time to time in order to see if you are on the right track.

Why The DASH Diet Promotes Fast Weight Loss?

In addition to all its other health benefits, the DASH diet supports healthy weight loss. This is one of the major reasons for its popularity. Although the DASH diet wasn't formulated primarily for weight loss, such as the Atkins and Paleo diets, among others, if accompanied by an exercise routine, it can facilitate quick and healthy weight loss.

The advantage of the DASH diet is that it helps in weight loss and simultaneously aims towards overall healthiness. It encompasses a systematic approach towards food intake, focusing on certain food choices that aid weight loss while avoiding foods that lead to weight gain. It can also help wean oneself off blood pressure and diabetes medications.

The DASH diet includes lots of vegetables and fruits in its meal plans. Fruits and vegetables are typically low in calories, high in fiber, and are satiating. A weight loss drink or supplement can help you lose weight; however, it will not satiate your hunger. Therefore you are likely to eat more frequently, so your calorie intake will go up.

The diet includes certain protein rich-foods at each meal orsnack that are likewise filling, avoiding either in-between meals or blood sugar crashes due to a sudden spike of insulin.

The meal plans of the DASH diet are not overloaded with carbohydrates. The plans are generally low on starchy foods, instead including protein rich-foods that prevent muscle breakdown and boost the metabolism for faster weight loss.

Should you need more information than is contained here, there is a plethora of books, articles and journals available online that can provide additional plans and menus. If followed rigorously, they can help you achieve your desired results.

Chapter 4: Health Benefits of Consuming Good Fats

The DASH diet comes with a range of health benefits. Following are some of the major advantages of following the DASH diet:

Cardiovascular Health

The DASH diet decreases your consumption of refined carbohydrates by increasing your consumption of foods high in potassium and dietary fiber (fruits, vegetables, and whole grains). In addition, it diminishes your consumption of saturated fats. Therefore, the DASH diet has a favorable effect on your lipid profile and glucose tolerance, which reduces the prevalence of metabolic syndrome (MS) in post-menopausal women.

Reports state that a diet limited to 500 calories favors a loss of 17% of total body weight in 6 months in overweight women. This reduces the prevalence of MS by 15%. However, when this diet follows the patterns of the DASH diet, while triglycerides decrease in a similar way, the reduction in weight and BP is even greater.

It also reduces blood sugar and increases HDL, which decreases the prevalence of MS in 35% of women. These results contrast with those of other studies, which have reported that the DASH diet alone, i.e., without caloric restriction, does not affect HDL and glycemia. This means that the effects of the DASH diet on MS are associated mainly with the greater reduction in BP and that, for more changes, the diet would be required to be combined with weight loss.

Helpful for Patients with Diabetes

The DASH diet has also been shown to help reduce inflammatory and coagulation factors (C-reactive protein and fibrinogen) in patients with diabetes. These benefits are associated with the contribution of antioxidants and fibers, given the high consumption of fruits and vegetables that the DASH diet requires. In addition, the DASH diet has been shown to reduce total cholesterol and LDL, which reduces the estimated 10-year cardiovascular risk. Epidemiological studies have determined that women in the highest quintile of food consumption according to the DASH diet have a 24% to 33% lower risk of coronary events and an 18% lower risk of a cerebrovascular event. Similarly, a meta-analysis of six observational studies has determined that the DASH diet can reduce the risk of cardiovascular events by 20%.

Weight Reduction

Limited research associates the DASH diet, in isolation, with weight reduction. In some studies, weight reduction was greater when the subject was on the DASH diet as compared to an isocaloric controlled diet. This could be related to the higher calcium intake and lower energy density of the DASH diet. The American guidelines for the treatment of obesity emphasize that, regardless of diet, a caloric restriction would be the most important factor in reducing weight.

However, several studies have made an association between (1) greater weight and fat loss in diets and (2) caloric restriction and higher calcium intake. Studies have also observed an inverse association between dairy consumption and body mass index (BMI). In obese patients, weight loss has been reported as being 170% higher after 24 weeks on a hypocaloric diet with high calcium intake.

In addition, the loss of trunk fat was reported to be 34% of the total weight loss as compared to only 21% in a control diet. It has also been determined that a calcium intake of 20 mg per gram has a protective effect in overweight middle-aged women. This would be equivalent to 1275 mg of calcium for a western diet of 1700 kcal. It has been suggested that low calcium intake increases the circulating level of the parathyroid hormone and vitamin D, which have been shown to increase the level of cytosolic calcium in adipocytes in vitro, changing the metabolism of lipolysis to lipogenesis.

Despite these reports, the effect that diet-provided calcium has on women's weight after menopause is a controversial subject. An epidemiological study has noted that a sedentary lifestyle and, to a lesser extent, caloric intake are associated with post-menopausal weight gain, though calcium intake is not associated with it. The average calcium intake in this group of women is approximately 1000 mg, which would be low, as previously stated. Another study of post-menopausal women shows that calcium and vitamin D supplementation in those with a calcium intake of less than 1200 mg per day decreases the risk of weight gain by 11%.

In short, the DASH diet is favorable, both in weight control and in the regulation of fatty tissue deposits, due to its high calcium content (1200 mg/day). The contribution of calcium apparently plays a vital role in the regulation of lipogenesis.

Now that we have established the myriad benefits of the DASH diet, let's check out some of the most delicious and unique DASH diet recipes for all times of the day!

Dash Food Groups Intake

All the DASH plans follow roughly this balance between the groups.

Grains:

The only source of processed food in DASH is grains, but these must be whole grains to conform to the diet. The reason for this is that they are higher in fiber and have less of an effect on blood sugar. Whole grain, steel-cut, and unbleached are what to look for on the label. Cereals, pasta, breads, and rice are all sources of grains but some are more processed than others. For example, granola is often less processed than a corn puff cereal. You can also try other grain substitutes like quinoa which also has a high protein content. A good rule is to stay away from any packaged food that looks white. White pasta, white bread, white flour etc., have all been refined and processed so they are essentially empty calories with no useful nutrition.

Vegetables:

Not all vegetables are created equal. Aim to buy fresh or frozen rather than tinned as these tend to be loaded with added sodium. Avoid any that come with sauces or added salt. Vegetables are a large part of DASH because your body needs fiber and vitamins but also because they are lower in calories. Some vegetables are not allowed on DASH because they cause high blood sugar spikes or are not nutritional enough. White potatoes are a prime example of this because they are heavy with starch which is then metabolized into pure sugar. Your body naturally metabolizes starches into sugars so you could be eating a sugary diet without even realizing it. Cruciferous greens and leafy greens are all advised on DASH as well as eating a colorful variety when possible.

Some vegetables, like beans, are actually legumes. These are perfect for DASH because they are high in protein and fiber without being animal products or being processed. If you're using canned beans look for low sodium and rinse them before use.

Dairy:

While many think that dairy is part of getting enough protein it's actually rather unnecessary. Swapping dairy for nut products is a good approach for DASH followers where possible. Dairy is allowed on DASH as long as it is low-fat with no added sugar. Many dairy products that are low-fat are pumped up with processed sugar to improve the taste. This means that even though the fat number is lower the calorie number is higher from the sugar. Yogurt is a prime example of this. Dairy can be a very filling choice, and it's also a supplemented source of vitamins D, B and A. Always read the ingredients on dairy products and avoid any with added hormones.

Fruits:

While fruits often get lumped together with vegetables, the DASH approach keeps them separate because you have to limit your intake. Most fruits are high in sugars which means that they cause your blood sugar to rise quickly. These are not allowed at all during phase one and only in a limited quantity during phase two. Despite the fact that fruits are often full of nutrients and fiber the amount they have does not balance out the huge levels of fructose and other natural sugars. Many processed fruits also have added sugar, making this worse. Dried and canned fruits are a prime example of this and should be avoided entirely. Fruit juice is also not recommended as it is literally a refined sugar cocktail.

Nuts & Seeds

These can be the perfect snacking item as they are rich in healthy fats and fiber. The problem with many nuts is that they are salted. This makes them wholly unsuitable for DASH. You'll also need to be careful with the serving size as they tend to be very calorie dense foods. Nut butters are a great alternative to sugary jams and an ideal snack food to include on DASH. Consider making your own or looking in the natural food section if you can't find ones without additives. Peanut butter can be especially problematic as many companies add xylitol to improve taste.

Animal Products

As you've seen it's important to limit animal products on DASH. Animals products like meat, eggs, and dairy all contain high amounts of cholesterol and saturated fat which is why they should be eaten in moderation only. Look for leaner cuts and grass-fed products where possible. A serving of any animal product should be limited to 3oz, this includes seafood. Avoid processed meat products like ham as they are pumped up with added salt to improve the flavor and help with preservation. It's a good idea to look at buying a slicer or making extra at dinner time so you can slice home cooked meats as "deli" leftovers instead which you know do not have added salt.

Fats

While not technically a food group fat are often added to foods to improve the taste or we use them to cook. Foods that are labeled as "fat-free" are often nothing more than a marketing ploy and may be loaded with sugar and much higher in calories. Your body and brain need fat to function so choosing unsaturated fats like avocado oil or coconut oil over more refined (canola) or animal fats (lard) is a much better choice. You can use grass fed butter for cooking as long as you include it in your daily allowance of animal products, the same goes for ghee. Avoid products that are heavily processed such as vegetable oils, margarine, shortening, frying oils and any that contain trans fats. Most trans-fats are difficult for the body to process and consuming them has been strongly linked to weight gain.

Chapter 5: Enhance your Results with Exercise

We all know that exercise is healthy but is it absolutely necessary in order to benefit from the DASH diet? Contrary to what many health advocates will tell you, going out of your way to exercise is not necessary for everyone. It depends on your own unique lifestyle. If you are a very active person or have a job that requires you to do a lot of manual labor, then chances are that you don't need to go out of your way to exercise. For example, if you work construction then going out of your way to exercise would be a bit repetitive since you get enough exercise working. However, if you work behind a desk then you probably need to take proactive steps to exercise.

The truth is that exercising, in combination with a healthy diet, will give you more energy and make you feel so much better! There are a lot of benefits to exercising that we're going to look at but just remember that you should always take things slowly. Don't start intense workouts immediately. You will need to work your way into it slowly.

Exercise Helps Control Weight

Exercise will help you control your weight because of its powerful impact on your metabolism. You'll prevent excess weight gain while also making it easier to lose weight in the first place. The truth is that while exercise is not a requirement in weight loss, it does make it so much easier.

You will burn calories when active. The more intense the activity, the more calories you will burn. While regular trips to the gym are highly beneficial, some people just can't afford to invest in the time required to be consistent so my advice is to find ways to become more active that fit into your everyday life. I will walk through a number of these methods later in the book.

Exercise Combats Disease and Other Health Conditions

DASH dieting is designed to help prevent high blood pressure so it's worth noting that exercise can actually enhance its effect. Exercise will also help prevent high blood pressure while also boosting your immune system. Furthermore, being active will boost your high-density lipoprotein (HDL) cholesterol which is also known as "good cholesterol." It also lowers those unhealthy triglycerides, known as "bad cholesterol."

Most doctors who prescribe DASH dieting will also encourage patients to exercise regularly. It's a powerful one-two punch!

Being active will also help prevent other health issues like stroke, metabolic syndrome, and even diabetes.

Exercise Improves your Mood

If you find yourself needing an emotional lift then you need look no further than exercise. A short session in the gym or a 30-minute walk will improve your mood. When you're physically active, a number of chemicals are released in the brain. These chemicals will make you happier and more relaxed.

Furthermore, exercise will help you feel better about your appearance so it boosts your confidence. Self-esteem is an important part of any lifestyle change. When you start growing confident in yourself, it becomes easier to stay consistent. You'll work harder on these improvements.

Exercise is the Best Energy Booster!

You might wonder how being physically active will actually give you more energy. After all, exercising results in fatigue – at least that's what most people believe. Regular activity will provide a boost to your muscle growth, therefore giving you a significant metabolic boost. That's why we tend to have more energy after a big workout.

Exercising allows your tissues to soak in oxygen, which improves your blood flow. In short, it gives you much more energy throughout the day. That's why exercising in the morning is so beneficial.

Exercise will Help you Sleep Better

If you are having trouble sleeping at night, then exercise is a solution! It helps you fall asleep faster and will even deepen your sleep. That's why people who have active jobs tend to get better sleep. Their schedule is consistent because they have no trouble falling asleep. They feel better and wake up earlier.

However, just make sure that you don't exercise too close to your bedtime. You will be too energized to fall asleep. Instead, an evening session should take place at least 4 hours prior to bed time.

Exercise is a Fun and Social Experience

There are a number of ways that you can enjoy the benefits of physical activity, many of which are quite enjoyable. So, don't limit yourself to spending hours on the treadmill or walking the same route every day. Try to engage in activities that you enjoy. Sports are a great way to get in your exercise while having a blast! Dance lessons are another!

Find activities that make you happy. That way you will be more likely to consistently follow through with them. If you get bored, then try something new.

How Often Should You Exercise?

First of all, you so not have to go out of your way to becoming more active. There are several ways that you can become more active. We're about to look at some of them, but for now just understand that you will need to aim for at least 100 minutes of moderate activity every week.

Try to make small changes so that your body has a chance to adapt and then slightly increase your activity until you hit your final goal. I do encourage at least two 30-minute weight training sessions per week since building your muscle mass provides you with a permanent metabolic boost. In other words, the more muscles you have, the more calories your body will burn throughout the day.

Simple Ways to Become More Active

It's easy to get swept away by our everyday lives. We call it "fast-paced" but for many, this life of all work and no play is mostly sitting behind a desk. While it is definitely busy work-wise, it's not exactly an active lifestyle. That's why it's important to take steps to add physical activity into our everyday life.

The following methods are an easy way to become more active in your everyday life. You'll start to become more mindful about these little things and turn everyday tasks into mini-workouts. You will be amazed at how much better you feel.

Walk More

Rather than driving two blocks to pick up the latest magazine from the magazine stand, walk those two blocks. This one simple decision will get you a 10-15-minute workout without having to go out of your way. You can also go for walks while chatting with your friend. Whatever it takes to walk more rather than just sitting around will help you become more active.

Take the Stairs Rather than the Elevator

Did you know that just five minutes of walking up the stairs can burn as many as 150 calories? If you work on an upper floor, then start walking up the stairs rather than taking the elevator. This is a small change where you don't really have to go out of your way to become more active. If you do these five times per week you have the potential to burn over 700 calories!

Clean More

Not only is having a clean house an amazing feeling, cleaning can burn up to 200 calories an hour. You should clean for at least one hour per week. Having a clean home is motivational and you will be killing two birds with one stone. Your home will be clean and you'll be burning 200 calories every week with no extra effort.

Use a Basket for Shopping Whenever Possible

If you are just making a short trip into the store, then you should use a basket rather than a cart. It's automatic for us to reach for a cart no matter what but when you use a basket, you're getting in an automatic weightlifting session. It can actually add up to quite the workout.

Park Further Away

While everyone else is fighting tooth and nail for those close parking spots, start parking further away so that you are forced to walk further. You will actually save a lot of time that you would have wasted looking for a close parking spot. Additionally, you will get in a mini workout by walking further.

Start Playing with your Pet

It goes without saying but if you have a dog, then you will have to go on frequent walks. So why not take it a step further by playing with your furry friend. Dogs are full of energy and will happily play games. You can get in a good workout while your dog stays happy! You can do the same thing with your cat. They also love to play but you'll usually have to initiate it. My point is that playing with your pet is an amazingly fun way to stay active.

Get Up At Least Once Every Hour

It's easy to lose track of time while working behind a desk so set an alarm to remind yourself to get up every hour. You should walk around or stretch for a minimum of two minutes before returning to your work. There are also programs like Break Pal that not only alert you when it's time to stand, but they give you a few simple tasks to perform before sitting back down.

The point that I am trying to make here is that small additions to your routine can make a huge difference. These changes will make it so that you don't have to go out of your way to exercise to become more active. Once you establish new habits, they become an automatic part of your everyday routine.

Exercises to Enhance the DASH Diet

For those of you who want to enhance the DASH diet even further, then you will want to include a few exercises into your daily routine. We'll look at some of the best workouts to include while DASH dieting.

Aerobic Exercise

Aerobic exercises will improve your circulation and help lower your blood pressure, making them the absolute best form of exercise to combine with DASH dieting. Additionally, it will help control how strongly your heart pumps blood and reduce the risk of type-2 diabetes.

Even if you already have diabetes, aerobic exercise will help your body control glucose levels.

Frequency: You should aim to exercise at least 120 minutes per week.

Examples of Aerobic Exercise

- Walking
- Running
- Swimming
- Cycling
- Sports
- Jump Rope

Strength Training

Strength training will have a more specific effect on the composition of your body. Individuals who are hauling around a lot of excess fat will find strength training to be quite beneficial to their weight loss efforts. Additionally, studies have shown that the combination of aerobic exercise and strength training actually lowers bad cholesterol levels while raising good cholesterol levels.

Frequency: Strength training workouts should be performed at least two days a week, making sure to rest for at least one day in between.

Examples of Strength Training Exercises

- Weightlifting
- Curling
- Resistance band workouts
- Push-ups
- Squats
- Pull-ups

Chapter 6: Breakfast Recipes

Sweet Avocado Smoothie

Preparation Time: 5 minutes

Cooking Time: 0 minutes

Servings: 2

Ingredients:

2 Cups Ice Cubes

1 Teaspoon Vanilla Extract, Pure

1 ½ Teaspoons Granulated Stevia 1 ½ Cups Milk, Nonfat

1 ½ Cups Peaches, Frozen

1 Cup Vanilla Greek Yogurt

1 Tablespoon Flaxseed, Ground

1 Avocado, Peeled & Pitted

Directions:

Blend all ingredients until smooth, and serve chilled.

Nutrition:

Calories: 323 Protein: 21 Grams Fat: 15 Grams

Carbs: 32 Grams Sodium: 142 mg Cholesterol: 9 mg

Cinnamon Apple Overnight Oats

Preparation Time: 8 hours and 15 minutes

Cooking Time: 0 minutes

Servings: 2

Ingredients:

1 Cup Old Fashioned Rolled Oats

2 Tablespoons Chia Seeds - 1 ¼ Cup Milk, Nonfat

½ Tablespoon Ground Cinnamon

2 Teaspoons Honey, Raw

½ Teaspoon Vanilla Extract, Pure

Dash Sea Salt

1 Apple, Diced

Directions:

Divide your chia seeds, oats, cinnamon, milk, honey, vanilla, and salt in mason jars. Place the lids on, and shake well until thoroughly combined. Remove the lids, and then add half of your diced apples to each jar. Sprinkle with cinnamon. Put the lids tightly back on the jars, and refrigerate overnight.

Nutrition: Calories: 339 Protein: 13 Grams Fat: 8 Grams

Carbs: 60 Grams Sodium: 66 mg Cholesterol: 3 mg

Blueberry Muffins

Preparation Time: 20 minutes

Cooking Time: 25 minutes

Servings: 12

Ingredients:

1 ¼ Cup Whole Wheat Flour

½ Cup Old Fashioned Rolled Oats

1 Teaspoon Baking Soda

1 Teaspoon Baking Powder

¼ Teaspoon Ground Cinnamon

¼ Teaspoon Sea Salt, Fine

¼ Cup Olive Oil

¼ Cup Dark Brown Sugar

1 Teaspoon Vanilla Extract, Pure

2 Eggs, Large

2/3 Cup Milk

1 Cup Blueberries, Fresh or Frozen

8 Medjool Dates, Pitted & Chopped

Directions:

Start by heating your oven to 350, and then line a muffin tin with liners.

Get out a bowl and stir your oats, flour, baking soda, baking powder, cinnamon and salt together until well combined.

Get out a different bowl and whisk your olive oil and brown sugar until the mixture turns fluffy. Whisk in the eggs one egg at a time until it's well beaten, and then add in your milk and vanilla extract. Beat to combine.

Pour your flour mixture with your wet ingredients, mixing well. Evenly spoon the batter between your muffin cups, and bake for twenty-five minutes. Allow to cool before storing.

Nutrition:

Calories: 180

Protein: 4 Grams

Fat: 6 Grams

Carbs: 30 Grams

Sodium: 172 mg

Cholesterol: 35 mg

Yogurt & Banana Muffins

Preparation Time: 15 minutes

Cooking Time: 25 minutes

Servings: 4

Ingredients:

3 Bananas, Large & Mashed

1 Teaspoon Baking Soda - 1 Cup Old Fashioned Rolled Oats

2 Tablespoons Flaxseed, Ground - 1 Cup Whole Wheat Flour

¼ Cup Applesauce, Unsweetened - ½ Cup Plain Yogurt

¼ Cup Brown Sugar - 2 Teaspoons Vanilla Extract, Pure

Directions:

Start by turning the oven to 355, and then get out a muffin tray. Grease it and then get out a bowl. Mix your flaxseed, oats, soda, and flour in a bowl. Mash your banana and then mix in your sugar, vanilla, yogurt and applesauce. Stir in your oats mixture, making sure it's well combined. It's okay for it to be lumpy. Divide between muffin trays, and then bake for twenty-five minutes. Serve warm.

Nutrition: Calories: 316 Protein: 11.2 Grams Fat: 14.5 Grams

Carbs: 36.8 Grams Sodium: 469 mg Cholesterol: 43 mg

Berry Quinoa Bowls

Preparation Time: 15 minutes

Cooking Time: 20 minutes

Servings: 2

Ingredients:

1 Small Peach, Sliced

2/3 + ¾ Cup Milk, Low Fat

1/3 Cup Uncooked Quinoa, Rinsed Well

½ Teaspoon Vanilla Extract, Pure

2 Teaspoons Brown Sugar - 14 Blueberries

2 Teaspoons Honey, Raw

12 Raspberries

Directions: Start to boil your quinoa, vanilla, 2/3 cup milk and brown sugar together for five minutes before reducing it to a simmer. Cook for twenty minutes. Heat a grill pan that's been greased over medium heat, and then add in your peaches to grill for one minute per side. Heat the remaining ¾ cup of milk in your microwave. Cook the quinoa with a splash of milk, berries and grilled peaches. Don't forget to drizzle with honey before serving it.

Nutrition: Calories: 435 Protein: 9.2 Grams Fat: 13.7 Grams

Carbs: 24.9 Grams Sodium: 141 mg Cholesterol: 78 mg

Pineapple Green Smoothie

Preparation Time: 5 minutes

Cooking Time: 0 minutes

Servings: 2

Ingredients:

1 ¼ Cups Orange Juice

½ Cup Greek Yogurt, Plain

1 Cup Spinach, Fresh

1 Cup Pineapple, Frozen & Chunked

1 Cup Mango, Frozen & Chunked

1 Tablespoons Ground Flaxseed

1 Teaspoon Granulated Stevia

Directions:

Start by blending everything together until smooth, and then serve cold.

Nutrition:

Calories: 213

Protein: 9 Grams Fat: 2 Grams Carbs: 43 Grams Sodium: 44 mg

Cholesterol: 2.5 mg

Peanut Butter & Banana Smoothie

Preparation Time: 5 minutes

Cooking Time: 0 minutes

Servings: 1

Ingredients:

1 Cup Milk, Nonfat

1 Tablespoons Peanut Butter, All Natural

1 Banana, Frozen & Sliced

Directions:

Start by blending everything together until smooth.

Nutrition:

Calories: 146

Protein: 1.1 Grams

Fat: 5.5 Grams

Carbs: 1.8 Grams

Mushroom Frittata

Preparation Time: 15 minutes

Cooking Time: 10 minutes

Servings: 4

Ingredients: 4 Shallots, Chopped - 1 Tablespoons Butter

2 Teaspoons parsley, Fresh & Diced - ½ lb. Mushrooms, Fresh & Diced - 3 Eggs

1 Teaspoon Thyme - 5 Egg Whites

¼ Teaspoon Black Pepper

1 Tablespoon Half & Half, Fat Free - ¼ Cup Parmesan Cheese, Grated

Directions:

Start by turning the oven to 350, and then get out a skillet. Grease it with butter, letting it melt over medium heat. Once your butter is hot adding in your shallots. Cook until golden brown, which should take roughly five minutes. Stir in your thyme, pepper, parsley and mushrooms. Beat your eggs, egg whites, parmesan, and half and half together in a bowl. Pour the mixture over your mushrooms, cooking for two minutes. Transfer the skillet to the oven, and bake for fifteen minutes. Slice to serve warm.

Nutrition: Calories: 391 Protein: 7.6 Grams Fat: 12.8 Grams

Carbs: 31.5 Grams Sodium: 32 mg Cholesterol: 112 mg

Cheesy Omelet

Preparation Time: 10 minutes

Cooking Time: 10 minutes

Servings: 4

Ingredients:

4 Eggs

4 Cups Broccoli Florets

1 Tablespoons Olive Oil

1 Cup Egg Whites

¼ Cup Cheddar, Reduced Fat

¼ Cup Romano, Grated

¼ Teaspoon Sea Salt, Fine

¼ Teaspoon Black Pepper

Cooking Spray as Needed

Directions:

Start by heating your oven to 350, and then steam your broccoli over boiling water for five to seven minutes. It should be tender.

Mash the broccoli into small pieces, and then toss with salt, pepper and olive oil.

Get out a muffin tray and then grease it with cooking spray. Divide your broccoli between the cups, and then get out a bowl.

In the bowl beat your eggs with salt, pepper, egg whites and parmesan.

Pour your batter over the broccoli, and then top with cheese. Bake for two minutes before serving warm.

Nutrition:

Calories: 427

Protein: 7.5 Grams

Fat: 8.6 Grams

Carbs: 13 Grams

Sodium: 282 mg

Cholesterol: 4.2 Grams

Ginger Congee

Preparation Time: 10 minutes

Cooking Time: 1 hour

Servings: 1

Ingredients:

1 Cup White Rice, Long Grain & Rinsed

7 Cups Chicken Stock

1 Inch Ginger, Peeled & Sliced Thin

Green Onion, Sliced for Garnish

Sesame Seed Oil to Garnish

Directions:

Start by boiling your ginger, rice and salt in a pot. Allow it to simmer and reduce to low heat. Give it a gentle stir, and then allow it to cook for an hour. It should be thick and creamy.

Garnish by drizzling with sesame oil and serving warm.

Nutrition:

Calories: 510

Protein: 13.5 Grams

Carbs: 60.7 Grams

Fat: 24.7 Grams Sodium: 840 mg Cholesterol: 0 mg

Egg Melts

Preparation Time: 10 minutes

Cooking Time: 10 minutes

Servings: 2

Ingredients:

1 Teaspoon Olive oil

2 English Muffins, Whole Grain & Split

4 Scallions, Sliced Fine

8 Egg Whites, Whisked

¼ Teaspoon Sea Salt, Fine

¼ Teaspoon Black Pepper

½ Cup Swiss Cheese, Shredded & Reduced Fat

½ Cup Grape Tomatoes, Quartered

Directions:

Set the oven to broil, and then put your English muffins on a baking sheet. Make sure the split side is facing up. Broil for two minutes. They should turn golden around the edges.

Get out a skillet and grease with oil. Place it over medium heat, and cook your scallions for three minutes.

Beat your egg whites with salt and pepper, and pour this over your scallions.

Cook for another minute, stirring gently.

Spread this on your muffins, and top with remaining scallions if desired, cheese and tomatoes. Broil for 1 and a half more minutes to melt the cheese and serve warm.

Nutrition:

Calories: 212

Protein: 5.3 Grams

Fat: 3.9 Grams

Carbs: 14.3 Grams

Sodium: 135 mg

Cholesterol: 0 mg

Fluffy Pancakes for Breakfast

Preparation Time: 10 minutes

Cooking Time: 10 minutes

Servings: 2

Ingredients:

Eggs – 1

Melted butter – 2 tablespoons

White vinegar – 2 tablespoons

Milk – 3/4 cup

All-purpose flour – 1 cup

Baking powder – 1 teaspoon

Baking soda – 1/2 teaspoon

White sugar – 2 tablespoons

Salt – 1/2 teaspoon

Cooking spray

Directions:

Begin with mixing milk and vinegar in a bowl and leave the solution for 5 minutes until it turns "sour".

Whip egg and butter together into the "soured" milk emulsion.

Add all-purpose flour, baking powder, baking soda, sugar, and salt in a separate bowl.

Take all the wet component and mix with the flour emulsion. Whisk the mixture until it becomes an even paste.

Take a frying pan and heat it over medium heat. Now coat the pan with cooking spray.

Take 1/4 cupful of the paste in a frying pan and cook well. Use a spatula to flip the cake and cook until it turns fluffy and golden brown.

Transfer the pancakes onto a plate and garnish with your choice of cream.

Nutrition:

Proteins: 6.4 g

Carbohydrates: 32.7 g

Fat: 8.2 g

Fluffy Zucchini Bread

Preparation Time: 20 minutes

Cooking Time: 1 hour

Servings: 24

Ingredients:

All-purpose white flour – 3 cups

Salt – 1 teaspoon

Baking soda – 1 teaspoon

Baking powder – 1 teaspoon

Cinnamon (ground) – – 1 teaspoon

Eggs – 3

Vegetable oil – 1 cup

Sugar – 2 1/4 cups

Vanilla extract – 3 teaspoons

Zucchini (grated) – 2 cups

Walnuts (chopped) – 1 cup

Directions:

Start by preheating the oven to 325 degrees F (165 degrees C).

Now grease two 9 x 5-inch pans or standard pans with cooking oil.

Flour the greased pans and remove the access flour.

Mix flour along with salt, baking powder, baking soda, and ground cinnamon.

In a separate bowl, take eggs, vegetable oil, sugar and vanilla extract and beat all the ingredients together.

Add dry flour mixture in the creamed solution and beat until it becomes a thick paste.

Grate two cups of zucchini.

Add grated zucchini and chopped walnuts in the paste and stir until all the ingredients are well combined in the flour paste.

Now pour the batter into the greased pans and bake for at least 40 to 60 minutes. Use a tester if required.

Let the bread cool in the pan until it is firm enough to be removed.

Cut into slices once the bread is completely cool.

Keep the remaining in the refrigerator.

Nutrition:

Proteins: 3.3 g

Carbohydrates: 32.1 g

Fat: 13.1 g

Spinach Crustless Quiche

Preparation Time: 20 minutes

Cooking Time: 30 minutes

Servings: 6

Ingredients:

Vegetable oil – 1 tablespoon

Chopped onion – 1

Frozen chopped spinach – 10 ounce/1 package

Eggs – 5

Muenster cheese (shredded) – 3 cups

Salt – 1/4 teaspoon

Black pepper (ground) – 1/8 teaspoon

Directions:

Begin with preheating the oven to 350 degrees F (175 degrees C).

Now grease a 9 x 5 inch pan or any standard pan with cooking oil.

Chop the onion and remove the frozen spinach in a strainer. Squeeze spinach to remove all the extra moisture or water.

Heat vegetable oil in a large frying pan and add chopped onion into it. Cook onions until they turn soft or light golden in color.

Add drained spinach into it and stir until moisture gets evaporated and remover the mixture.

Take eggs in a fresh bowl and whip. Add salt, cheese, and pepper into it.

Now take the spinach mixture and add to the whipped egg solution and stir until everything is blended well.

Pour mixture into the greased pan and bake in the oven for 30 minutes.

Leave the dish until it cools and serve by cutting into slices of your choice

Nutrition:

Proteins: 20.4 g

Carbohydrates: 4.8 g

Fat: 23.7 g

Friendly French Toast

Preparation Time: 10 minutes

Cooking Time: 20 minutes

Servings: 12

Ingredients:

All-purpose flour – 1/4 cup

Milk – 1 cup

Salt – 1/2 teaspoon

Eggs – 3

Cinnamon (ground)– 1/2 teaspoon

Vanilla extract – 1 teaspoon

Sugar – 1 tablespoon

Bread – 12 slices

Directions: Take all-purpose flour in a bowl and add milk, eggs, salt (as per taste) and ground cinnamon, vanilla extract, and sugar. Whisk the mixture to make a smooth paste. Take a frying pan and heat it lightly. Take a slice of bread and soak it completely in the paste. Repeat this with all the slices. Now cook each slice of bread until it turns golden brown on both sides. Serve hot with maple syrup.

Nutrition: Proteins: 4.8 g Carbohydrates: 19.4 g Fat: 2.7 g

Everyday Crepes

Preparation Time: 10 minutes

Cooking Time: 20 minutes

Servings: 4

Ingredients:

All-purpose flour – 1 cup

Eggs – 2

Milk – 1/2 cup

Water – 1/2 cup

Salt – 1/4 teaspoon

Butter (melted) – 2 tablespoons

Directions:

Start by taking all-purpose flour in a mixing bowl and or milk, water, salt, eggs and whisk together to make a running paste.

Add melted butter to the paste.

Heat a frying pan on medium flame and add a quarter cup of the batter into it.

Spread the batter evenly in the frying pan and let the crepe cook on both the sides. Serve hot.

Nutrition: Proteins: 7.4 g   Carbohydrates: 25.5 g   Fat: 9.2 g

Hash Brown Cheesy Ham Casserole

Preparation Time: 15 minutes

Cooking Time: 1 hour

Servings: 12

Ingredients:

Hash brown potatoes (frozen package) – 1

Diced ham (cooked) – 8 ounces

Cream of potato soup (condensed) – 2 cans

Sour cream – 1

Cheddar cheese (shredded) – 2 cups

Parmesan cheese (grated) – 1 1/2 cups

Directions:

Start by preheating the oven to 375 degrees F (190 degrees C).

In a fresh bowl, take frozen packaged mix hash browns potatoes, diced cooked ham, shredded cheddar cheese, sour cream, and condensed cream of potato soup. Mix all the ingredients evenly. Now grease a large 9x13 inch baking dish and spread the mixture into it. Sprinkle grated parmesan cheese to cover the mixture evenly in the baking dish. Bake the dish in the oven for an hour until it is light brown in color. Serve hot garnished with parmesan cheese

Nutrition: Proteins: 14.4 g Carbohydrates: 29.7 g Fat: 27.2 g

Baffle Waffles

Preparation Time: 10 minutes

Cooking Time: 15 minutes

Servings: 5

Ingredients::

All-purpose flour – 2 cups

Salt – 1 teaspoon

Baking powder – 4 teaspoons

Sugar – 2 tablespoons

Eggs – 2

Milk (warm) – 1 1/2 cups

Butter (melted) – 1/3 cup

Vanilla extract – 1 teaspoon

Directions:

Start by preheating the waffle iron to your desired set temperature.

Now take a fresh large bowl and add two cups of all-purpose flour, one teaspoon of salt, four teaspoons of baking powder and two teaspoons of sugar.

Stir all the ingredients in the mixture together and keep it aside.

Now take a third of a cup of butter and melt it.

Now in a fresh bowl take two eggs and mix with warm milk, melted butter and one teaspoon of vanilla extract.

Empty the mixture into the flour mixture and whisk it well to create a slurpy batter.

Now grease the preheated waffle iron and pour the batter evenly on it.

Close the waffle iron and cook until waffles turn crispy golden.

Top the waffle with whipped cream, maple syrup or fruit of your choice and serve hot.

Nutrition:

Proteins: 10.2 g

Carbohydrates: 47.6

Fat: 16.2

Banana Sour Cream Bread

Preparation Time: 10 minutes

Cooking Time: 1 hour

Servings: 32

Ingredients:

Sugar – 3 cups

Cinnamon (ground) – 1 teaspoon

Butter – 3/4 cup

Eggs – 3

Ripe bananas (mashed) – 6

Sour cream – 1 container

Vanilla extract – 2 teaspoons

Cinnamon (ground) – 2 teaspoons

Salt – 1/2 teaspoon

Baking soda – 3 teaspoons

All-purpose flour – 4 1/2 cups

Chopped walnuts (optional) – 1 cup

Directions:

Start by preheating the oven to 300 degrees F (150 degrees C).

Take two large loaf pans and grease evenly

Take a small bowl and add 1/4 cup white sugar, 1 teaspoon ground cinnamon and stir them together.

Now take the cinnamon and sugar mixture and dust spray the greased loaf pans.

Take a fresh bowl and add ripe bananas to mash well.

In a separate bowl take 3/4 cup of butter and three cups of white sugar. Mix them well.

Add three eggs to the same bowl, mashed bananas and mix them well.

Now add 16 ounces of sour cream, and two teaspoons of vanilla extract and two teaspoons of ground cinnamon and stir it well.

Add half teaspoon of salt, three teaspoons baking soda and four cups of all-purpose flour to the bowl. Stir to make a paste. You can also add walnuts to the paste (Optional). Mix them well into the batter. Now evenly spread the batter in the greased large loaf pans and bake well for one hour.

Insert a toothpick in the center of the pans to check if the bread is baked properly. Cut into slices and serve. Put the remaining bread in the refrigerator.

Nutrition: Proteins: 3.7 g Carbohydrates: 40.1 g Fat: 10.4 g

Cinnamon Baked Bread

Preparation Time: 15 minutes

Cooking Time: 35 minutes

Servings: 15

Ingredients:

Refrigerated biscuit dough – 3 packages

Sugar – 1 cup

Cinnamon (ground) – 2 teaspoons

Margarine – 1/2 cup

Brown sugar – 1 cup

Chopped walnuts (optional) – 1/2 cup

Raisins – 1/2 cup

Directions:

Start by preheating the oven to 350 degrees F (175 degrees C).

Take a hard surface 9-inch Bundt pan and grease well with cooking spray.

Now take a cup of sugar and two teaspoons of ground cinnamon in a resealable plastic bag. Mix them well together.

Take three packets of refrigerated biscuits dough and cut each dough piece into small quarters.

Add at least 8 chopped biscuit dough pieces in the sugar-cinnamon mixture.

Seal the plastic bag and shake well until the dough pieces get evenly coated in sugar-cinnamon mixture.

Put a layer of sugar-cinnamon coated pieces in the bottom of the greased Bundt pan.

You can also add chopped walnuts and raisins over the layer to get the crunchy flavor. This step is totally optional.

Continue with a layer of sugar-cinnamon dough in the Bundt pan.

Take a frying pan pour half a cup of margarine and a cup of brown sugar.

Cook the mixture until margarine is completely melted and mixed well with sugar to form a smooth thick paste. Let the mixture boil for two minutes.

Now evenly pour the mixture over the biscuit dough placed inside Bundt pan.

Bake the bread in the preheated oven (350 degrees F) for 35 minutes until it turns puffy and golden brown.

Remove the pan and let the bread cool in Bundt pan for at least 10 minutes.

Once cooled, flip the Bundt pan and remove the bread onto a plate.

Nutrition: Proteins: 5.3 g Carbohydrates: 61.5 g Fat: 17.7 g

Buttermilk Pancake

Preparation Time: 15 minutes

Cooking Time: 10 minutes

Servings: 12

Ingredients:

All-purpose flour – 3 cups

White sugar – 3 tablespoons

Baking powder – 3 teaspoons

Baking soda – 1 1/2 teaspoons

Salt – 3/4 teaspoon

Buttermilk – 3 cups

Milk – 1/2 cup

Eggs – 3

Butter (melted) – 1/3 cup

Directions:

Begin with preheating the to 200 degrees F.

In a fresh bowl take three cups of all-purpose, three tablespoons of sugar, three teaspoons of baking powder, 1 1/2 teaspoons of baking soda, and 3/4 teaspoon salt and stir it well.

Take a fresh bowl and add three large eggs, three cups of buttermilk, 1/2 cup of milk, and 1/3 cup of butter and stir them well together.

Now empty the mixture in the flour mixture and mix well until the batter turns slightly lumpy. Avoid making it too thin or too thick.

Take a large frying pan and heat it on medium flame.

Brush the pan with the butter using a scapula.

Use half cup batter and pour over the hot pan. Turn the batter upside down with a spatula once each side is evenly golden brown in color.

Remove the cakes on a plate and transfer them in the preheated oven to stay warm.

Use the remaining batter to make cakes.

Once cooked, serve hit with maple syrup or spread of your choice.

Nutrition:

Proteins: 7.2 g

Carbohydrates: 30.7 g

Fat: 7.4 g

French Toast with Blueberries

Preparation Time: 15 minutes

Cooking Time: 1 hour and 15 minutes

Servings: 10

Ingredients:

Day-old bread – 12 slices

Cream cheese – 2 packages

Fresh blueberries – 1 cup

Eggs – 12

Milk – 2 cups

Vanilla extract – 1 teaspoon

Maple syrup – 1/3 cup

White sugar – 1 cup

Cornstarch – 2 tablespoons

Water – 1 cup

Blueberries – 1 cup

Butter– 1 tablespoon

Directions:

Take a 9x13 inch baking dish and evenly grease it with cooking spray.

Now cut 12 slices of day-old small bread into one-inch cube each.

Take half of the sliced bread cubes in the baking dish

Now cut two eight once of packages of creamed cheese into one-inch cubes and put them nicely over the layer of arranged bread cubes in the baking dish. Take one cup of fresh blueberries and sprinkle them over bread cubes on cream cheese. Top the blueberries with remaining pieces of bread cubes. Now take a fresh large bowl and break 12 eggs into it and beat nicely. Add two cups of milk, one teaspoon of vanilla extract and 1/3 cup of maple syrup in the bowl with beaten eggs. Now mix all the ingredients together. Take the mixture and pour evenly over the cubed bread mixture. Ensure that the bread cubes are nicely dipped in the liquid mixture. Now cover the mixture with an aluminum foil and refrigerate the mixture overnight. Remove the bowl from the refrigerator at least half an hour before baking the next day. Now preheat the oven to 350 degrees F (175 degrees C). Put the baking dish in the oven and bake for 30 minutes. Now remove the aluminum foil from the baking dish and bake for another 30 minutes. Now take a fresh pan and add a cup of sugar, two tablespoons of cornstarch, and one cup of water. Mix the solution and boil while continuously stirring the mixture. Cook for at least 3 minutes. Mix a cup of fresh blueberries to the heated syrup and simmer the haet as the blueberries begin to burst and leave color. Add one tablespoon of butter in the mixture and pour the blueberries sauce over the baked toast. Cut into pieces and serve with maple syrup or the blueberries sauce.

Nutrition: Proteins: 15.1 g Carbohydrates: 51.1 g Fat: 24.8

Plumpy Pumpkin Bread

Preparation Time: 15 minutes

Cooking Time: 1 hour

Servings: 36

Ingredients:

Canned pumpkin puree – 3 cups

Vegetable oil – 1 1/2 cups

Sugar – 4 cups

Eggs – 6

All-purpose flour – 4 3/4 cups

Baking powder – 1 1/2 teaspoons

Baking soda – 1 1/2 teaspoons

Salt – 1 1/2 teaspoons

Cinnamon (ground) – 1 1/2 teaspoons

Nutmeg (ground) – 1 1/2 teaspoons

Cloves (ground) – 1 1/2 teaspoons

Directions:

Start by preheating the oven to 350 degrees F (175 degrees C).

Now take three 9x5 inch loaf pans and grease them using regular cooking spray.

Evenly spray all-purpose flour pan on the greased loaf pans and set them aside.

Now take a fresh large bowl and add 6 eggs into it. Beat them gently into a paste.

Add three cups of canned pumpkin puree, 1 ½ cups of vegetable oil, and four cups of sugar in the bowl with beaten eggs and mix well to form a thick paste.

Now take a big bowl and add 4 3/4 cups of all-purpose flour, 1 ½ teaspoon of baking powder, 1 ½ teaspoon of baking soda, and 1 ½ teaspoon of salt, 1 ½ teaspoon of ground cinnamon, 1 ½ teaspoon of nutmeg, and 1 ½ teaspoon of ground cloves.

Whisk all the ingredients together and add to the pumpkin paste. Stir the mixture until it is evenly blended.

Now place the batter evenly in the greased loaf pans.

Once done, put the greased loaf pans in the preheated oven and bake for at least 50 minutes.

Use a toothpick inserted in the center of the dish to check if it is properly baked or not. Remove the loaf pans from the oven and let it cool for 15-20 minutes. Cut into slices and serve with creamed cheese or nuts of your liking.

Nutrition: Proteins: 3 g Carbohydrates: 36.8 g Fat: 10.3 g

Vintage Pancakes

Preparation Time: 5 minutes

Cooking Time: 15 minutes

Servings: 8

Ingredients: All-purpose flour – 1 ½ cups

Baking powder – 3 ½ teaspoons

Salt – 1 teaspoon - S ugar – 1 tablespoon

Milk – 1 ¼ cups - Egg – 1

Butter (melted) – 3 tablespoons

Directions: Begin by taking 1 ½ cups of all-purpose flour in a big fresh bowl. Add 3 ½ teaspoons of baking powder, 1 teaspoon of salt, and 1 teaspoon of sugar into the flour bowl. Now create space in the center of the flour mixture and pour 1 ¼ cups of milk, one egg, and three tablespoons of melted butter. Mix all the ingredients together until you get a smooth batter. Now take a medium frying pan and heat it spraying a little oil over it. Take a quarter cup full f batter and spread over the medium heated frying pan. Spread the batter evenly without leaving any lumps. Heat the cake until the sides start turning golden brown. Flip the pancake using a spatula once you see little bubbles on the surface of the cake. Serve the pancakes hot with a topping of your choice or maple syrup.

Nutrition: Proteins: 4.5 g Carbohydrates: 21.7 g Fat: 5.9 g

Pampered Zucchini Bread

Preparation Time: 20 minutes

Cooking Time: 1 hour

Servings: 24

Ingredients:

All-purpose flour – 3 cups

Salt – 1 teaspoon

Baking soda – 1 teaspoon

Baking powder – 1 teaspoon

Cinnamon (ground) – 3 tablespoon

Eggs – 3

Vegetable oil – 1 cup

Regular sugar – 2 ¼ cups

Vanilla extract – 3 teaspoons

Zucchini (grated) – 2 cups

Walnuts (chopped) – 1 cup

Directions:

Start by preheating the oven to 325 degrees F (165 degrees C).

Now grease a 9 x 4 inch standard baking pans with cooking spray.

Now spray all-purpose flour over the baking pans. Remove any access amount of flour.

Take a fresh medium bowl and add three cups of all-purpose flour, one teaspoon of salt, one teaspoon of baking soda, one teaspoon of baking powder, and three tablespoons of ground cinnamon together.

Now take a fresh big bowl and break three eggs into it.

Add one cup of vegetable oil to the egg bowl along with 2 ¼ cups of regular sugar and a tablespoon of vanilla extract. Beat together all the ingredients in the mixture.

Now empty the all-purpose flour mixture into the beaten egg mixture and stir well to form a thick paste of batter.

Grate three medium-sized zucchini, one cup of chopped walnuts and add to the prepared all-flour batter and stir well.

Now pour the batter evenly into prepared baking pans.

Put the pans in the preheated oven and bake the dish for about 50 minutes.

Use a toothpick to check if the dish is properly baked.

Let the cake cool in the pan for 20 minutes before removing the cake in the pan. Cut into slices of your choice. Leave the remaining cake in the refrigerator.

Nutrition: Proteins: 3.3 g Carbohydrates: 32.1 g Fat: 13.1 g

Chapter 7: Lunch Recipes

Shrimp Quesadillas

Preparation Time: 16 minutes

Cooking Time: 5 minutes

Servings: 2

Ingredients:

Two whole wheat tortillas

½ tsp. ground cumin

4 cilantro leaves - 3 oz. diced cooked shrimp

1 de-seeded plump tomato

¾ c. grated non-fat mozzarella cheese

¼ c. diced red onion

Directions: In medium bowl, combine the grated mozzarella cheese and the warm, cooked shrimp. Add the ground cumin, red onion, and tomato. Mix together. Spread the mixture evenly on the tortillas. Heat a non-stick frying pan. Place the tortillas in the pan, then heat until they crisp. Add the cilantro leaves. Fold over the tortillas. Press down for 1 – 2 minutes. Slice the tortillas into wedges. Serve immediately.

Nutrition: Calories: 99 Fat: 9 g

Carbs: 7.2 g Protein: 59 g Sugars: 4 g Sodium: 500 mg

The OG Tuna Sandwich

Preparation Time: 15 minutes

Cooking Time: 5 minutes

Servings: 2

Ingredients:

30 g olive oil

1 peeled and diced medium cucumber

2 ½ g pepper

4 whole wheat bread slices

85 g diced onion

2 ½ g salt

1 can flavored tuna   - 85 g shredded spinach

Directions: Grab your blender and add the spinach, tuna, onion, oil, salt and pepper in, and pulse for about 10 to 20 seconds. In the meantime, toast your bread and add your diced cucumber to a bowl, which you can pour your tuna mixture in. Carefully mix and add the mixture to the bread once toasted. Slice in half and serve, while storing the remaining mixture in the fridge.

Nutrition: Calories: 302 Fat: 5.8 g

Carbs: 36.62 g Protein: 28 g Sugars: 3.22 g Sodium: 445 mg

Easy To Understand Mussels

Preparation Time: 10 minutes

Cooking Time: 10 minutes

Servings: 4

Ingredients:

2 lbs. cleaned mussels

4 minced garlic cloves

2 chopped shallots

Lemon and parsley

2 tbsps. Butter

½ c. broth

½ c. white wine

Directions: Clean the mussels and remove the beard Discard any mussels that do not close when tapped against a hard surface Set your pot to Sauté mode and add chopped onion and butter Stir and sauté onions Add garlic and cook for 1 minute Add broth and wine Lock up the lid and cook for 5 minutes on HIGH pressure Release the pressure naturally over 10 minutes Serve with a sprinkle of parsley and enjoy!

Nutrition: Calories: 286 Fat: 14 g

Carbs: 12 g Protein: 28 gSugars: 0g Sodium: 314 mg

Chili-Rubbed Tilapia with Asparagus & Lemon

Preparation Time: 10 minutes

Cooking Time: 10 minutes

Servings: 4

Ingredients:

3 tbsps. Lemon juice

2 tbsps. Chili powder

2 tbsps. Extra-virgin olive oil

½ tsp. divided salt

2 lbs. trimmed asparagus

½ tsp. garlic powder

1 lb. tilapia fillets

Directions:

Bring 1 inch of water to a boil in a large saucepan. Put asparagus in a steamer basket, place in the pan, cover and steam until tender-crisp, about 4 minutes.

Transfer to a large plate, spreading out to cool.

Combine chili powder, garlic powder and ¼ teaspoon salt on a plate. Dredge fillets in the spice mixture to coat. Heat oil in a large nonstick skillet over medium-high heat. Add the fish and cook until just opaque in the center, gently turning halfway, and 5 to 7 minutes total.

Divide among 4 plates. Immediately add lemon juice, the remaining ¼ teaspoon salt and asparagus to the pan and cook, stirring constantly, until the asparagus is coated and heated through, about 2 minutes.

Serve the asparagus with the fish.

Nutrition:

Calories: 211

Fat: 10 g

Carbs: 8 g

Protein: 26 g

Sugars: 0.4 g

Sodium: 375.7 mg

Parmesan-Crusted Fish

Preparation Time: 5 minutes

Cooking Time: 7 minutes

Servings: 4

Ingredients:

¾ tsp. ground ginger

1/3 c. panko bread crumbs

Mixed fresh salad greens

¼ c. finely shredded parmesan cheese

1 tbsp. butter

4 skinless cod fillets

3 c. julienned carrots

Directions:

Preheat oven to 450 °F. Lightly coat a baking sheet with nonstick cooking spray.

Rinse and pat dry fish; place on baking sheet. Season with salt and pepper.

In small bowl stir together crumbs and cheese; sprinkle on fish.

Bake, uncovered, 4 to 6 minutes for each 1/2-inch thickness of fish, until crumbs are golden and fish flakes easily when tested with a fork.

Meanwhile, in a large skillet bring 1/2 cup water to boiling; add carrots. Reduce heat.

Cook, covered, for 5 minutes. Uncover; cook 2 minutes more. Add butter and ginger; toss.

Serve fish and carrots with greens.

Nutrition:

Calories: 216.4

Fat: 10.1 g

Carbs: 1.3 g

Protein: 29.0 g

Sugars: 0.1 g

Sodium: 428.3 mg

Lemony Braised Beef Roast

Preparation Time: 15 minutes

Cooking Time: 6-8 hours

Servings: 6

Ingredients:

1 tbsp. minced fresh rosemary

½ c. low-fat, low-sodium beef broth

Freshly ground black pepper

2 lbs. lean beef pot roast

1 sliced onion

2 minced garlic cloves

¼ c. fresh lemon juice

1 tsp. ground cumin

Directions:

In a large slow cooker, add all ingredients and mix well.

Set the slow cooker on low.

Cover and cook for about 6-8 hours.

Nutrition: Calories: 344 Fat: 2.8 g

Carbs: 18 g Protein: 32 g Sugars: 2.4 g Sodium: 278 mg

Grilled Fennel-cumin Lamb Chops

Preparation Time: 10 minutes

Cooking Time: 15 minutes

Servings: 2

Ingredients:

¼ tsp. salt

1 minced large garlic clove

1/8 tsp. cracked black pepper

¾ tsp. crushed fennel seeds

¼ tsp. ground coriander

4-6 sliced lamb rib chops

¾ tsp. ground cumin

Directions: Trim fat from chops. Place the chops on a plate. In a small bowl combine the garlic, fennel seeds, cumin, salt, coriander, and black pepper. Sprinkle the mixture evenly over chops; rub in with your fingers. Cover the chops with plastic wrap and marinate in the refrigerator at least 30 minutes or up to 24 hours. Grill chops on the rack of an uncovered grill directly over medium coals until chops are desired doneness.

Nutrition: Calories: 239 Fat: 12 g

Carbs: 2 g Protein: 29 g Sugars: 0 g Sodium: 409 mg

Beef Heart

Preparation Time: 40 minutes

Cooking Time: 30 minutes

Servings: 4

Ingredients:

1 chopped large onion

1 c. water

2 peeled and chopped tomatoes

1 boiled beef heart

2 tbsps. tomato paste

Directions:

Boil the beef heart until half-done.

Sauté the onions with tomatoes until soft.

Cut the beef heart into cubes and add to tomato and onion mixture. Add water and tomato paste. Stew on low heat for 30 minutes.

Nutrition: Calories: 138 Fat: 3 g Carbs: 0.1 g

Protein: 24.2 g

Sugars: 0 g

Sodium: 50.2 mg

Jerk Beef and Plantain Kabobs

Preparation Time: 10 minutes

Cooking Time: 15 minutes

Servings: 4

Ingredients:

2 peeled and sliced ripe plantains

2 tbsps. Red wine vinegar

Lime wedges

1 tbsp. cooking oil - 1 sliced medium red onion

12 oz. sliced boneless beef sirloin steak

1 tbsp. Jamaican jerk seasoning

Directions: Trim fat from meat. Cut into 1-inch pieces. In a small bowl, stir together red wine vinegar, oil, and jerk seasoning. Toss meat cubes with half of the vinegar mixture. On long skewers, alternately thread meat, plantain chunks, and onion wedges, leaving a 1/4-inch space between pieces. Brush plantains and onion wedges with remaining vinegar mixture. Place skewers on the rack of an uncovered grill directly over medium coals. Grill for 12 to 15 minutes or until meat is desired doneness, turning occasionally. Serve with lime wedges.

Nutrition: Calories: 260 Fat: 7 g

Carbs: 21 g Protein: 26 g Sugars: 2.5 g Sodium: 358 mg

Beef Pot

Preparation Time: 10 minutes

Cooking Time: 40 minutes

Servings: 2

Ingredients:

4 tbsps. Sour cream

¼ shredded cabbage head

1 tsp. butter

2 peeled and sliced carrots

1 chopped onion

10 oz. boiled and sliced beef tenderloin

1 tbsp. flour

Directions:

Sauté the cabbage, carrots and onions in butter.

Spray a pot with cooking spray.

In layers place the sautéed vegetables, then beef, then another layer of vegetables. Beat the sour cream with flour until smooth and pour over the beef. Cover and bake at 400F for 40 minutes.

Nutrition: Calories: 210 Fat: 30 g

Carbs: 4 g Protein: 14 g Sugars: 1 g Sodium: 600 mg

Cheesy Black Bean Wraps

Preparation Time: 10 minutes

Cooking Time: 5 minutes

Servings: 6

Ingredients:

2 Tablespoons Green Chili Peppers, Chopped

4 Green Onions, Diced

1 Tomato, Diced

1 Tablespoon Garlic, Chopped

6 Tortilla Wraps, Whole Grain & Fat Free

¾ Cup Cheddar Cheese, Shredded

¾ Cup Salsa

1 ½ Cups Corn Kernels

3 Tablespoons Cilantro, Fresh & Chopped

1 ½ Cup Black Beans, Canned & Drained

Directions:

Toss your chili peppers, corn, black beans, garlic, tomato, onions and cilantro in a bowl.

Heat the mixture in a microwave for a minute, and stir for a half a minute.

Spread the two tortillas between paper towels and microwave for twenty seconds. Warm the remaining tortillas the same way, and add a half a cup of bean mixture, two tablespoons of salsa and two tablespoons of cheese for each tortilla. Roll them up before serving.

Nutrition:

Calories: 341

Protein: 19 Grams

Fat: 11 Grams

Carbs: 36.5 Grams

Sodium: 141 mg

Cholesterol: 0 mg

Arugula Risotto

Preparation Time: 10 minutes

Cooking Time: 15 minutes

Servings: 4

Ingredients:

1 Tablespoon Olive Oil

½ Cup Yellow Onion, Chopped

1 Cup Quinoa, Rinsed

1 Clove Garlic, Minced

2 ½ Cups Vegetable Stock, Low Sodium

2 Cups Arugula, Chopped & Stemmed

1 Carrot, Peeled & shredded

½ Cup Shiitake Mushrooms, Sliced

¼ Teaspoon Black Pepper

¼ Teaspoon Sea Salt, Fine

¼ Cup Parmesan Cheese, Grated

Directions:

Get a saucepan and place it over medium heat, heating up your oil. Cook for four minutes until your onions are softened, and then add in your garlic and quinoa. Cook for a minute.

Stir in your stock, and bring it to a boil. Reduce it to simmer, and cook for twelve minutes.

Add in your arugula, mushrooms and carrots, cooking for an additional two minutes.

Add in salt, pepper and cheese before serving.

Nutrition:

Calories: 288

Protein: 6 Grams

Fat: 5 Grams

Carbs: 28 Grams

Sodium: 739 mg

Cholesterol: 0.5 mg

Vegetarian Stuffed Eggplant

Preparation Time: 20 minutes

Cooking Time: 15 minutes

Servings: 2

Ingredients:

4 Ounces White Beans, Cooked

1 Tablespoons Olive Oil

1 cup Water

1 Eggplant

¼ Cup Onion, Chopped

½ Cup Bell Pepper, Chopped

1 Cup Canned Tomatoes, Unsalted

¼ Cup Tomato Liquid

¼ Cup Celery, Chopped

1 Cup Mushrooms, Fresh & Sliced

¾ Cup Breadcrumbs, Whole Wheat

Black Pepper to Taste

Directions:

Preheat the oven to 350, and then grease a baking dish with cooking spray.

Trim the eggplant and cut it in half lengthwise. Scoop the pulp out using a spoon, leaving a shell that's a quarter of an inch thick.

Place the shells in the baking dish with their cut side up.

Add the water to the bottom of the dish, and dice the eggplant pulp into cubes, setting them to the side.

Add the oil into an iron skillet, heating it over medium heat.

Stir in peppers, chopped eggplants, and onions with your celery, mushrooms, tomatoes and tomato juice.

Cook for ten minutes on simmering heat, and then stir in your bread crumbs, beans and black pepper. Divide the mixture between eggshells.

Cover with foil, and bake for fifteen minutes. Serve warm.

Nutrition:

Calories: 334

Protein: 26 Grams

Fat: 10 Grams

Carbs: 35 Grams

Sodium: 142 mg

Cholesterol: 162 mg

Vegetable Tacos

Preparation Time: 15 minutes

Cooking Time: 15 minutes

Servings: 4

Ingredients:

1 Tablespoon Olive Oil

1 Cup Red Onion, Chopped

1 Cup Yellow Summer Squash, Diced

1 Cup Green Zucchini, Diced

3 Cloves Garlic, Minced

4 Tomatoes, Seeded& Chopped

1 Jalapeno Chili, Seeded & Chopped

1 Cup Corn Kernels, Fresh

1 Cup Pinto Beans, Canned, Rinsed & Drained

½ Cup Cilantro, Fresh & Chopped

8 Corn Tortillas

½ Cup Smoke Flavored Salsa

Directions:

Get out a saucepan and add in your olive oil over medium heat, and stir in your onion. Cook until softened.

Add in your squash and zucchini, cooking for an additional five minutes.

Stir in your garlic, beans, tomatoes, jalapeño and corn. Cook for an additional five minutes before stirring in your cilantro and removing the pan from heat.

Warm each tortilla, in a nonstick skillet for twenty seconds per side.

Place the tortillas on a serving plate, spooning the vegetable mixture into each. Top with salsa, and roll to serve.

Nutrition:

Calories: 310

Protein: 10 Grams

Fat: 6 Grams

Carbs: 54 Grams

Sodium: 97 mg

Cholesterol: 20 mg

Fruit Chicken Salad

Preparation Time: 45 minutes

Cooking Time: 45 minutes

Servings: 8

Ingredients:

Boneless chicken breast halves – 4 skinless

Diced stalk celery – 1 cup

Green onions – 4

Golden apple – 1

Golden raisins – 1/3 cup

Seedless green grapes – 1/3 cup

Chopped toasted pecans – 1/2 cup

Ground black pepper – 1/8 teaspoon

Curry powder – 1/2 teaspoon

Light mayonnaise – 3/4 cup

Directions:

Start by taking four boneless chicken breast halves and cut them into equal tiny cubes.

Now take a pan and cook chicken cubes well. Do not overcook.

Take four green onions and chop them into pieces.

One cup of thin-sliced diced stalk celery, four chopped green onions, one peeled golden apple, 1/3 cup of golden raisins, 1/3 cup of seedless green grapes chopped in two halves, 1/2 cup of chopped toasted pecans, 1/8 teaspoon of ground black pepper, 1/2 teaspoon of Curry powder

Now lightly mix all ingredients put into the bowl. Avoid mashing.

Keep the bowl aside for at least two minutes.

Now add 3/4 cup of light mayonnaise in the bowl and gently mix the mixture. Ensure that the spread is evenly divided

Cover the bowl with plastic film and put it in the refrigerator for half an hour.

Serve before it gets soggy.

The salad tastes well when kept overnight.

Nutrition:

Calories: 229

Proteins: 15.1 g

Carbohydrates: 12.3 g

Fat: 14 g

Whole Grain Pasta with Meat Sauce

Preparation Time: 10 minutes

Cooking Time: 30 minutes

Servings: 6

Ingredients:

Whole-grain pasta – 1 pound

Extra-lean ground beef – 1 pound

Onion – 1, diced

Garlic – 3 cloves, minced

No-salt-added tomato sauce – 2 (8-ounce) cans

Red wine – 1/3 cup

Balsamic vinegar – 1 Tbsp.

Dried basil - 1 tsp.

Dried marjoram – ½ tsp.

Dried oregano – ½ tsp.

Dried red pepper flakes - ½ tsp.

Dried thyme - ½ tsp.

Freshly ground black pepper - ½ tsp.

Directions:

Follow the direction on the package and cook the pasta. Omit the salt. Drain and set aside.

Place onion, ground beef and garlic in a pan over medium heat. Stir-fry for 5 minutes, or until the beef has browned.

Add remaining ingredients and stir to combine. Simmer, uncovered, for 10 minutes, stirring occasionally.

Remove from heat and spoon over pasta.

Serve.

Nutrition:

Calories: 387

Fat: 5g

Carb: 58g

Protein: 27g

Sodium 65mg

Beef Tacos

Preparation Time: 10 minutes

Cooking Time: 20 minutes

Servings: 6

Ingredients:

Extra-lean ground beef – 1 pound

Large onion – 1, chopped

Garlic – 2 cloves, minced

No-salt-added tomato sauce – 1 (8-ounce) can

Low-sodium Worcestershire sauce – 2 tsp.

Molasses - 1 Tbsp.

Apple cider vinegar – 1 Tbsp.

Ground cumin – 1 Tbsp.

Ground sweet paprika – 1 Tbsp.

Dried red pepper flakes - ½ tsp.

Ground black pepper to taste

Low-sodium taco shells – 1 package

Chopped fresh cilantro - ¼ cup

Tomato and lettuce of serving

Directions:

Place the ground beef, onion, and garlic in a pan over medium heat.

Stir-fry for 5 minutes or until the beef is browned.

Lower heat to medium-low and add the Worcestershire sauce, tomato sauce, molasses, vinegar, cumin, red pepper flakes, paprika, and black pepper. Simmer, stirring frequently, about 10 minutes.

Heat taco shells according to package directions. Set aside.

Remove the sauté pan from the heat. Stir in cilantro.

Divide evenly between the taco shells.

Garnish with lettuce, tomato and serve.

Nutrition:

Calories: 255

Fat: 9g

Carb: 23g

Protein: *18*g

Sodium 79mg

Dirty Rice

Preparation Time: 10 minutes

Cooking Time: 30 minutes

Servings: 4

Ingredients:

Extra-lean ground beef - ½ pound

Large onion – 1, diced

Celery – 2 stalks, diced

Garlic – 2 cloves, minced

Bell pepper – 1, diced

Sodium-free beef bouillon granules - 1 tsp.

Water - 1 cup

Low-sodium Worcestershire sauce – 2 tsp.

Dried thyme – 1 ½ tsp.

Dried basil – 1 tsp.

Dried marjoram - ½ tsp.

Ground black pepper - ¼ tsp.

Pinch ground cayenne pepper

Scallions – 2, diced

Cooked long-grain brown rice – 3 cups

Directions:

In a pan, place the onion, ground beef, celery, and garlic. Stir-fry for 5 minutes or until beef is browned.

Add beef bouillon, bell pepper, water, sauce, and herbs and stir to combine.

Bring to a boil.

Then reduce heat to low, and cover.

Simmer for 20 minutes.

Stir in the scallions and simmer, uncovered, for 3 minutes.

Remove from heat. Add cooked rice and stir to combine.

Serve.

Nutrition:

Calories: 272

Fat: 4g

Carb: 41g

Protein: 16g

Sodium 92mg

Beef with Pea Pods

Preparation Time: 5 minutes

Cooking Time: 10 minutes

Servings: 4

Ingredients:

Thin beef steak – ¾ pound, sliced into thin strips

Peanut oil – 1 Tbsp.

Scallions – 3, sliced

Garlic – 2 cloves, minced

Minced fresh ginger – 2 tsp.

Fresh pea pods – 4 cups, trimmed

Homemade soy sauce – 3 Tbsp.

Cooked brown rice – 4 cups

Directions:

Heat the oil in a pan. Add the garlic, scallions, and ginger. Stir-fry for 30 seconds. Add the sliced beef and stir-fry for 5 minutes, or until beef has browned. Add pea pods and soy sauce and stir-fry for 3 minutes. Remove from heat. Serve with rice.

Nutrition: Calories: 466 Fat: 11g Carb: 64g Protein: 27g Sodium 71mg

Whole-Grain Rotini with Ground Pork

Preparation Time: 10 minutes

Cooking Time: 25 minutes

Servings: 6

Ingredients:

Whole-grain rotini - 1 (13-ounce) package

Lean ground pork – 1 pound

Red onion – 1, chopped

Garlic – 3 cloves, minced

Bell pepper – 1, chopped

Pumpkin puree – 1 cup

Ground sage – 2 tsp.

Ground rosemary – 1 tsp.

Ground black pepper to taste

Directions: Cook the pasta (follow the package insturctions). Omit salt, drain and set aside. Heat a pan over medium heat. Add onion, garlic, and ground pork and sauté for 2 minutes. Add bell pepper and sauté for 5 minutes. Remove from heat. Add pasta to the pan along with remaining ingredients. Mix and serve.

Nutrition: Calories: 331 Fat: 7g Carb: 45g Protein: 23g Sodium 48mg

Roasted Pork Loin with Herbs

Preparation Time: 20 minutes

Cooking Time: 1 hour

Servings: 4

Ingredients:

Boneless pork loin roast – 2 lbs.

Garlic – 3 cloves, minced

Dried rosemary – 1 Tbsp.

Dried thyme – 1 tsp.

Dried basil – 1 tsp.

Salt – ¼ tsp.

Olive oil – ¼ cup

White wine – ½ cup

Pepper to taste

Directions:

Preheat the oven to 350F.

Crush the garlic with thyme, rosemary, basil, salt, and pepper, making a paste. Set aside.

Use a knife to pierce meat several times.

Press the garlic paste into the slits.

Rub the meat with the rest of the garlic mixture and olive oil.

Place pork loin into the oven, turning and basting with pan liquids, until the pork reaches 145F, about 1 hour. Remove the pork from the oven.

Place the pan over heat and add white wine, stirring the brown bits on the bottom.

Top roast with sauce.

Serve.

Nutrition:

Calories: 464

Fat: 20.7g

Carb: 2.4g

Protein: 59.6g

Sodium 279mg

Garlic Lime Pork Chops

Preparation Time: 20 minutes

Cooking Time: 10 minutes

Servings: 4

Ingredients:

Lean boneless pork chops – 4 (6-oz. each)

Garlic – 4 cloves, crushed

Cumin – ½ tsp.

Chili powder - ½ tsp.

Paprika - ½ tsp.

Juice of ½ lime

Lime zest – 1 tsp.

Kosher salt - ¼ tsp.

Fresh pepper to taste

Directions: In a bowl, season pork with cumin, chili powder, paprika, garlic salt, and pepper. Add lime juice and zest. Marinate the pork for 20 minutes. Line a broiler pan with foil. Place the pork chops on the broiler pan and broil for 5 minutes on each side or until browned. Serve.

Nutrition:

Calories: 233 Fat: 13.2g Carb: 4.3g Protein: 25.5g Sodium 592mg

Lamb Curry with Tomatoes and Spinach

Preparation Time: 10 minutes

Cooking Time: 12 minutes

Servings: 4

Ingredients:

Olive oil – 1 tsp.

Lean boneless lamb – 1 pound, sliced thinly

Onion – 1, chopped

Garlic – 3 cloves, minced

Red bell pepper – 1, chopped

Salt-free tomato paste – 2 Tbsp.

Salt-free curry powder – 1 Tbsp.

No-salt-added diced tomatoes – 1(15-ounce) can

Fresh baby spinach – 10 ounces

Low-sodium beef or vegetable broth - ½ cup

Red wine – ¼ cup

Chopped fresh cilantro – ¼ cup

Ground black pepper to taste

Directions:

Heat the oil in a pan.

Add lamb and brown both sides, about 2 minutes.

Add garlic, onion, and bell pepper. Stir-fry for 2 minutes. Stir in the curry powder and tomato paste.

Add the tomatoes with juice, spinach, broth, and wine and stir to mix.

Stir-fry for 3 to 4 minutes and lamb has cooked through.

Remove from heat. Season with pepper and stir in cilantro.

Serve.

Nutrition:

Calories: 238

Fat: 7g

Carb: 14g

Protein: 27g

Sodium 167mg

Pomegranate-Marinated Leg of Lamb

Preparation Time: 10 minutes

Cooking Time: 20 minutes

Servings: 6

Ingredients:

Bottled pomegranate juice - ½ cup

Hearty red wine – ½ cup

Ground cumin - 1 tsp.

Dried oregano – 1 tsp.

Crushed hot red pepper – ½ tsp.

Garlic – 3 cloves, minced

For the lamb

Boneless leg of lamb – 1 ¾ pound, butterflied and fat trimmed

Kosher salt – ½ tsp.

Olive oil spray

Directions:

To make the marinade, whisk everything in a bowl and transfer to a zippered plastic bag.

To prepare the lamb: add the lamb to the bag, press out the air, and close the bag. Marinate for 1 hour in the refrigerator.

Preheat the broiler (8 inches from the source of heat).

Remove the lamb from the marinade, blot with paper towels, but do not dry completely.

Season with salt. Spray the broiler rack with oil.

Place the lamb on the rack and broil, turning occasionally, about 20 minutes, or until lamb is browned and reaches 130F.

Remove from heat, slice and serve with carving juices on top.

Nutrition:

Calories: 273

Fat: 15g

Carb: 0g

Protein: 31g

Sodium 219mg

Beef Fajitas with Peppers

Preparation Time: 10 minutes

Cooking Time: 12 minutes

Servings: 6

Ingredients:

Olive oil – 2 tsp. plus more for the spray

Sirloin steak – 1 pound, cut into bite-size pieces

Red bell pepper – 1, chopped

Green bell pepper – 1, chopped

Red onion – 1, chopped

Garlic - 2 cloves, minced

DASH friendly Mexican seasoning – 1 Tbsp. (or any seasoning without salt)

Boston lettuce leaves – 12 for serving

Lime wedges or corn tortillas for serving

Directions:

Heat oil in a skillet.

Add half of the sirloin and cook until browned on both sides, about 2 minutes. Transfer to a plate.

Then repeat with the remaining sirloin.

Heat the 2 tsp. oil in the skillet.

Add onion, bell peppers, and garlic, cook and stir for 7 minutes or until tender.

Stir in the beef with any juices and the seasoning. Transfer to a plate.

Fill lettuce lead with beef mixture and drizzle lime juice on top.

Roll up and serve.

Nutrition:

Calories: 231

Fat: 12g

Carb: 6g

Protein: 24g

Sodium 59mg

Chapter 8: Dinner Recipes

Pork Medallions with Herbs de Provence

Preparation Time: 5 minutes

Cooking Time: 10 minutes

Servings: 2

Ingredients:

Pork tenderloin – 8 ounces, cut into 6 pieces (crosswise)

Ground black pepper to taste

Herbs de Provence – ½ tsp.

Dry white wine – ¼ cup

Directions:

Season the pork with black pepper.

Place the pork between waxed paper sheets and roll with a rolling pin until about ¼ inch thick.

Cook the pork in a pan for 2 to 3 minutes on each side.

Remove from heat and season with the herb. Place the pork on plates and keep warm. Cook the wine in the pan until boiling. Scrape to get the brown bits from the bottom. Serve pork with the sauce.

Nutrition: Calories: 120 Fat: 2g Carb: 1g Protein: 24g Sodium 62mg

Baked Chicken

Preparation Time: 10 minutes

Cooking Time: 1 hour

Servings: 4

Ingredients:

Chicken – 3 to 4 pound, cut into parts

Olive oil – 3 Tbsp.

Thyme – ½ tsp.

Sea salt – ¼ tsp.

Ground black pepper

Low-sodium chicken stock – ½ cup

Directions:

Preheat the oven to 400F.

Rub oil over chicken pieces. Sprinkle with salt, thyme, and pepper.

Place chicken in the roasting pan.

Bake in the oven for 30 minutes.

Then lower the heat to 350F.

Bake for 15 to 30 minutes more or until juice runs clear. Serve.

Nutrition: Calories: 550 Fat: 19g Carb: 0g Protein: 91g Sodium 480mg

Orange Chicken and Broccoli Stir-Fry

Preparation Time: 10 minutes

Cooking Time: 15 minutes

Servings: 4

Ingredients:

Olive oil – 1 Tbsp.

Chicken breast – 1 pound, boneless and skinless, cut into strips

Orange juice – 1/3 cup

Homemade soy sauce - 2 Tbsp.

Cornstarch – 2 tsp.

Broccoli – 2 cups, cut into small pieces

Snow peas – 1 cup - Cabbage – 2 cups, shredded

Brown rice – 2 cups, cooked - Sesame seeds – 1 Tbsp.

Directions: Combine the orange juice, soy sauce, and corn starch in a bowl. Set aside. Heat oil in a pan. Add chicken. Stir-fry until the chicken is golden brown on all sides, about 5 minutes. Add snow peas, cabbage, broccoli, and sauce mixture. Continue to stir-fry for 8 minutes or until vegetables are tender but still crisp.

Nutrition:

Calories: 340 Fat: 8g Carb: 35g Protein: 28g Sodium 240mg

Mediterranean Lemon Chicken and Potatoes

Preparation Time: 10 minutes

Cooking Time: 30 minutes

Servings: 4

Ingredients:

Chicken breast – 1 ½ pound, skinless and boneless, cut into 1-inch cubes

Yukon Gold potatoes – 1 pound, cut into cubes

Onion – 1, chopped

Red pepper – 1, chopped

Low-sodium vinaigrette – ½ cup

Lemon juice – ¼ cup

Oregano – 1 tsp.

Garlic powder – ½ tsp.

Chopped tomato – ½ cup

Ground black pepper to taste

Directions:

Preheat oven to 400F.

Except for the tomatoes, mix everything in a bowl.

On 4 aluminum foils, place an equal amount of chicken and potato mixture. Fold to make packets.

Bake at 400F for 30 minutes. Open packets.

Top with chopped tomatoes.

Season with black pepper to taste.

Nutrition:

Calories: 320

Fat: 4g

Carb: 34g

Protein: 43g

Sodium 420mg

Tandoori Chicken

Preparation Time: 10 minutes

Cooking Time: 20 minutes

Servings: 6

Ingredients:

Nonfat yogurt – 1 cup, plain

Lemon juice – ½ cup

Garlic – 5 cloves, crushed

Paprika – 2 Tbsp.

Curry powder – 1 tsp.

Ground ginger – 1 tsp.

Red pepper flakes – 1 tsp.

Chicken breasts – 6, skinless and boneless, cut into 2-inch chunks

Wooden skewers – 6, soaked in water

Directions:

Preheat the oven to 400F.

In a bowl, combine lemon juice, yogurt, garlic, and spices. Blend well.

Divide chicken and thread onto skewers. Place skewers in a baking dish.

Pour half of the yogurt mixture onto chicken. Cover and marinate in the refrigerator for 20 minutes

Spray a baking dish with cooking spray.

Place chicken skewers in the pan and coat with the remaining ½ of yogurt marinade.

Bake in the oven until chicken is cooked, about 15 to 20 minutes.

Serve with veggies or brown rice.

Nutrition:

Calories: 175

Fat: 2g

Carb: 8g

Protein: 30g

Sodium 105mg

Mighty Garlic and Butter Sword Fish

Preparation Time: 10 minutes

Cooking Time: 2 hours and 30 minutes

Servings: 4

Ingredients:

½ c. melted butter

6 chopped garlic cloves

1 tbsp. black pepper

5 sword fish fillets

Directions:

Take a mixing bowl and toss in all of your garlic, black pepper alongside the melted butter

Take a parchment paper and place your fish fillet in that paper

Cover it up with the butter mixture and wrap up the fish

Repeat the process until all of your fish are wrapped up

Let it cook for 2 and a half hours and release the pressure naturally

Serve

Nutrition: Calories: 379

Fat: 26 g Carbs: 1 g Protein: 34 g Sugars: 0 g Sodium: 666 mg

Supreme Cooked Lobster

Preparation Time: 10 minutes

Cooking Time: 7 minutes

Servings: 4

Ingredients:

1 c. white wine

1 c. water

2 lobster pieces

Directions:

Add the listed ingredients to your Instant Pot

Lock up the lid and cook on HIGH pressure for 7 minutes

Release the pressure naturally

Open and add some extra melted butter

Serve and enjoy!

Nutrition:

Calories: 231

Fat: 9 g

Carbs: 5 g

Protein: 30 g Sugars: 0 g Sodium: 551 mg

Tilapia with Parsley

Preparation Time: 10 minutes

Cooking Time: 1 hour and 30 minutes

Servings: 6

Ingredients:

2 tbsps. Melted low-fat unsalted butter

1 tsp. garlic powder

¼ c. chopped fresh parsley

Freshly ground black pepper

4 oz. tilapia fillets

3 tsps. Grated fresh lemon rind

Directions:

Grease a slow cooker.

Sprinkle the tilapia fillets with garlic powder and black pepper generously.

Place lemon rind and parsley over fillets evenly.

Drizzle with melted butter. Set the slow cooker on low. Cover and cook for about 1½ hours.

Nutrition: Calories: 239.1 Fat: 4.3 g Carbs: 22.3 g Protein: 33.7 g

Sugars: 0 g Sodium: 381 mg

Thai Coconut Tilapia and Rice

Preparation Time: 15 minutes

Cooking Time: 25 minutes

Servings: 4

Ingredients:

170 g chopped baby spinach

425 g coconut milk

2 ½ g salted butter

680 g jasmine

2 ½ g chili flakes

4 coconut crusted tilapia fillets

680 g coconut water

Directions:

Preheat the oven to 400 oF and place fish in a lightly greased pan. Bake for 25 minutes.

In the meantime, put your rice in a pot to cook with coconut water, coconut milk, and a dash of salt. Set the pot at medium heat for about 2 minutes, till it reaches boiling point, then put the heat down and let the rice simmer for about twenty more minutes.

Add the chili flakes in now, to allow the rice to fully take in the flavor. Just before you are ready to serve, add in the spinach and stir for about 3 to 4 minutes, before straining both, and plating.

Take the fish out of the oven, slice, and serve over the coconut rice.

Nutrition:

Calories: 190

Fat: 3.4 g

Carbs: 35.67 g

Protein: 6 g

Sugars: 1.7 g

Sodium: 256.2 mg

Nutmeg Pork Chops

Preparation Time: 10 minutes

Cooking Time: 35 minutes

Servings: 3

Ingredients:

1 chopped yellow onion

1 tbsp. balsamic vinegar

½ c. organic olive oil

3 boneless pork chops

8 oz. sliced mushrooms

2 tsps. Ground nutmeg

¼ c. coconut milk

1 tsp. garlic powder

Directions: Heat up a pan using the oil over medium heat, add mushrooms and onions, stir and cook for 5 minutes. Add pork chops, nutmeg and garlic powder and cook for 5 minutes more. Add vinegar and coconut milk, toss, introduce inside oven and bake at 350 oF and bake for a half-hour. Divide between plates and serve.   Enjoy!

Nutrition: Calories: 260

Fat: 10 gCarbs: 8 g Protein: 22 g Sugars: 2.4 g Sodium: 78 mg

Butter and Dill Pork Chops

Preparation Time: 5 minutes

Cooking Time: 26 minutes

Servings: 4

Ingredients:

½ c. chicken broth

½ c. white wine

4 bone-in pork loin pieces

2 tbsps. unflavored vinegared butter

1 tbsp. minced fresh dill fronds

½ tsp. flavored vinegar

½ tsp. ground black pepper

16 baby carrots

Directions:

The first step here is to set your pot to sauté mode

Season the chops with pepper and flavored vinegar

Toss your chops into your pot and cook for 4 minutes

Transfer the chops to a plate and repeat to cook and brown the rest

Pour in 1 tablespoon of butter and Toss in your carrots, dill to the cooker and let it cook for about 1 minute

Pour in the wine and scrape off any browned bits in your cooker while the liquid comes to a boil

Stir in the broth

Return the chops to your pot

Lock up the lid and let it cook for about 18 minutes at high pressure

Naturally release the pressure by keeping it aside for 8 minutes

Unlock and serve with some sauce poured over

Nutrition:

Calories: 296

Fat: 25 g

Carbs: 0 g

Protein: 17 g

Sugars: 1.3 g

Sodium: 155 mg

Paprika Pork with Carrots

Preparation Time: 10 minutes

Cooking Time: 30 minutes

Servings: 4

Ingredients:

1 sliced red onion

1 lb. cubed pork stew meat

2 tbsps. olive oil

¼ c. low-sodium veggie stock

Black pepper

2 peeled and sliced carrots

2 tsps. sweet paprika

Directions:

Heat up a pan with the oil over medium heat, add the onion, stir and sauté for 5 minutes.

Add the meat, toss and brown for 5 minutes more.

Add the rest of the ingredients, bring to a simmer and cook over medium heat for 20 minutes. Divide the mix between plates and serve.

Nutrition: Calories: 328

Fat: 18.1 g Carbs: 6.4 g Protein: 34 g Sugars: 14 g Sodium: 399 mg

Pork and Greens Mix

Preparation Time: 10 minutes

Cooking Time: 20 minutes

Servings: 4

Ingredients:

4 oz. mixed salad greens

1 tbsp. chopped chives

1/3 c. coconut aminos

2 tbsps. balsamic vinegar

1 tbsp. olive oil

4 oz. sliced pork stew meat

1 c. halved cherry tomatoes

Directions:

Heat up a pan with the oil over medium heat, add the pork, aminos and the vinegar, toss and cook for 15 minutes.

Add the salad greens and the other ingredients, toss, cook for 5 minutes more, divide between plates and serve.

Nutrition:

Calories: 125 Fat: 6.4 g

Carbs: 6.8 g Protein: 9.1 g Sugars: 0.2 g Sodium: 388.6 mg

Sage Pork Chops

Preparation Time: 10 minutes

Cooking Time: 35 minutes

Servings: 4

Ingredients:

2 tbsps. olive oil

1 tbsp. lemon juice

4 pork chops

1 tbsp. chopped sage

Black pepper

1 tsp. smoked paprika

2 minced garlic cloves

Directions:

In a baking dish, combine the pork chops with the oil and the other ingredients, toss, introduce in the oven and bake at 400 oF for 35 minutes.

Divide the pork chops between plates and serve with a side salad.

Nutrition: Calories: 263

Fat: 12.4 g Carbs: 22.2 g Protein: 16 g Sugars: 0 g Sodium: 960 mg

Pork with Avocados

Preparation Time: 10 minutes

Cooking Time: 15 minutes

Servings: 4

Ingredients:

1 c. halved cherry tomatoes

½ c. low-sodium veggie stock

1 tbsp. olive oil

2 c. baby spinach

1 lb. sliced pork steak

2 peeled, pitted and sliced avocados

1 tbsp. balsamic vinegar

Directions:

Heat up a pan with the oil over medium-high heat, add the meat, toss and cook for 10 minutes.

Add the spinach and the other ingredients, toss, cook for 5 minutes more, divide into bowls and serve.

Nutrition: Calories: 390

Fat: 12.5 g Carbs: 16.8 g Protein: 13.5 g Sugars: 1 g Sodium: 0 mg

Simple Roast

Preparation Time: 10 minutes

Cooking Time: 45 minutes

Servings: 6

Ingredients:

3 Cloves Garlic, Minced

Black Pepper to Taste

1 Cup Beef Stock, Low Sodium

2 Yellow Onions, Chopped Roughly

4 lbs. Chuck Roast, Lean & Fat Removed

1 Thyme Sprig, Fresh & Chopped

2 Carrots, Sliced

3 Bay Leaves

2 Celery Stalks, Chopped

Directions:

Mix everything in your instant pot and then seal the lid. Cook on high pressure for forty-five minutes, and then slice the roast to serve.

Nutrition:

Calories: 351 Protein: 14 Grams Fat: 7 Grams Carbs: 20 Grams

Easy Chili

Preparation Time: 10 minutes

Cooking Time: 15 minutes

Servings: 4

Ingredients:

1 Tablespoon Chili Powder

1 Tablespoon Cumin

1 lb. Chicken, Ground

2 Cloves Garlic, Minced

1 Tablespoon Avocado Oil

1 Yellow Onion, Chopped

1 Teaspoon Cocoa Powder

2 Tablespoons Tomato Paste

1 Cup Chicken Stock, Low Sodium

1 Teaspoon Oregano

2 Cups Corn

Black Pepper to Taste

28 Ounces Tomatoes, Canned & No Salt

28 Ounces Kidney Beans, Canned, No Salt, Drained & Rinsed

Directions:

Mix everything together in your instant pot and then stir well. Seal the lid, and cook on high pressure for fifteen minutes.

Finish with a quick release and then serve warm.

Nutrition:

Calories: 265

Protein: 7 Grams

Fat: 6 Grams

Carbs: 19 Grams

Italian Shrimp Dinner

Preparation Time: 15 minutes

Cooking Time: 15 minutes

Servings: 4

Ingredients:

8 Ounces Mushrooms, Chopped

1 lb. Shrimp, Peeled & Deveined

1 Yellow Onion, Chopped

1 Asparagus Bunch, Chopped

Black Pepper to Taste

2 Tablespoons Olive Oil

2 Teaspoons Italian Seasoning

1 Teaspoon Red Pepper Flakes, Crushed

1 Cup Cheddar Cheese, Fat Free & Grated

2 Cloves Garlic, Minced

1 Cup Coconut Cream

1 Cup Water

Directions:

Add the steamer basket to your instant pot after filling with one cup water.

Add the asparagus in the basket, and seal the lid. Cook on high pressure for three minutes, and then use a quick release. Submerge it in ice water to stop the asparagus from cooking, and drain before setting it aside.

Clean the instant pot and then press sauté. Add oil, and once it' shot cook your onion and mushrooms for four minutes. Add pepper flakes, Italian seasoning and the asparagus back in. stir well, and cook for a few minutes.

Add the cheddar, garlic, shrimp and coconut cream. Cover and cook on high pressure for four minutes. Serve warm.

Nutrition:

Calories: 275

Protein: 8 Grams

Fat: 6 Grams

Carbs: 17 Grams

Cabbage & Beef Stew

Preparation Time: 1 hour and 14 minutes

Cooking Time: 16 minutes

Servings: 6

Ingredients:

4 Carrots, Chopped

4 Cups Water

1 Cabbage Head, Shredded

3 Cloves Garlic, Chopped

Black Pepper to Taste

2 Bay Leaves

2 ½ lbs. Beef Brisket, Fat Removed

Directions:

Place your brisket in the instant pot with water, pepper, bay leaves and garlic. Seal the lid and cook on high pressure for one hour.

Use a quick release, and then add the cabbage, carrot, and stir well. Cook on high pressure for six minutes, and then use a natural pressure release for ten minutes. Follow with a quick release and serve warm.

Nutrition: Calories: 281 Protein: 8 Grams Fat: 8 Grams

Carbs: 21 Grams

Fish Curry

Preparation Time: 10 minutes

Cooking Time: 10 minutes

Servings: 6

Ingredients:

2 Onions, Sliced

2 Cloves Garlic, Minced

6 Curry Leaves

14 Ounces Coconut Milk

1 Tomato, Chopped

1 Tablespoon Olive Oil

6 White Fish Fillets, Skinless, Boneless & Chopped

1 Tablespoon Coriander, Ground

1 Tablespoon Ginger, Grated

½ Teaspoon Turmeric

Black Pepper to taste

2 Tablespoons Lemon Juice, Fresh

½ Teaspoon Fenugreek, Ground

Directions:

Press sauté and add the curry leaves and oil. Fry for a minute before adding the garlic, coriander, onion, ginger, turmeric, coconut milk, tomatoes, fish and fenugreek. Stir well, and then seal the lid.

Cook on low pressure for ten minutes before using a quick release.

Add the black pepper and stir well. Serve drizzled with lemon juice.

Nutrition:

Calories: 281

Protein: 7 Grams

Fat: 6 Grams

Carbs: 14 Grams

Beef Bourguignon

Preparation Time: 10 minutes

Cooking Time: 30 minutes

Servings: 4

Ingredients:

1 lb. Stewing Steak

½ lb. Bacon

5 Carrots

1 Red Onion, Sliced

2 Cloves Garlic, Minced

2 Teaspoon Rock Flavored Vinegar

2 Tablespoons Thyme, Fresh

2 Tablespoons Parsley, Fresh

2 Teaspoon Black Pepper

1 Tablespoon Olive Oil

½ Cup Beef Broth

Directions:

Set your pot to sauté and heat up the tablespoon of oil.

Once it's hot add the beef in batches to brown on all sides, and then place your beef to the side.

Slice your cooked bacon and add it to the strips. Add the strips bac into the pot with your onion, and then brown for three minutes.

Throw in the remaining ingredients, and seal the lid.

Cook on high pressure for thirty minutes, and then allow for a natural pressure release for ten minutes. Enjoy warm.

Nutrition:

Calories: 416

Protein: 18 Grams

Fats: 18 Grams

Carbs: 12 Grams

Lobster Bisque

Preparation Time: 10 minutes

Cooking Time: 10 minutes

Servings: 4

Ingredients:

1 Teaspoon Black Pepper

1 Teaspoon Dill, Dried

32 Ounces Chicken Broth, Low Sodium

1 Tablespoon Butter

2 Shallots, Minced

1 Clove Garlic, Minced

1 Cup Celery, Diced

1 Cup Carrots, Diced

29 Ounces Tomatoes, Diced

½ Teaspoon Paprika

4 Lobster Tails

1 Pint Heavy Whipping Cream

Directions:

Add in the garlic, shallots and butter in a microwave safe bowl. Microwave for three minutes before adding in the tomatoes, celery, carrot, garlic and shallots. Add it all into your instant pot.

Add in the broth and spices, and then use a knife to cut the lobster tails.

Lock the lid and cook on high pressure for four minutes. Use a natural pressure release for ten minutes followed by a quick release.

Use an immersion blender, and blend until smooth.

Nutrition:

Calories: 437

Protein: 38 Grams

Fat: 17 Grams

Carbs: 21 Grams

Pineapple Spicy Shrimp

Preparation Time: 3 minutes

Cooking Time: 12 minutes

Servings: 4

Ingredients:

¼ Cup Dry White Wine

2 Tablespoons Soy Sauce

2 Tablespoon Thai Sweet Chili Sauce

1 lb. Shrimp, Large

1 Tablespoon Ground Chili Paste

½ Cup Pineapple Juice, Unsweetened - 12 Ounces Quinoa

1 Red Bell Pepper, Large & Sliced

Directions: Drain your juice from the pineapple, and set it to the side. Measure ½ a cup of juice out. Mix together the bell pepper, pineapple juice, rice, wine, chili sauce, soy sauce, chopped scallions and chili paste in the bottom of your instant pot. Put the shrimp on top before locking the lid. Cook on high pressure for two minutes before using a natural pressure release for ten minutes. Follow with a quick release. Serve garnished with pineapple chunks and scallions.

Nutrition: Calories: 299 Protein: 8 Grams Fat: 5 Grams Carbs: 54 Grams

Seafood & Chickpea Pot

Preparation Time: 5 minutes

Cooking Time: 20 minutes

Servings: 4

Ingredients:

2 Cod Fillets

2 Cups Vegetable Broth

2 Tablespoons Black Pepper

1 lb. Shrimp

1 Cup Scallions, Chopped - 1 Carrot, Chopped

1 Cup Chickpea, Soaked & Drained

1 Tomato, Chopped for Garnish

¼ Cup Cheese for Garnish

Directions: Throw in all ingredients into your instant pot, and then seal the lid. Cook on high pressure for twelve minutes. Allow for a natural pressure release for ten minutes before following it with a quick release. Top with cheese and tomatoes before serving. Cheddar cheese is recommended.

Nutrition: Calories: 268 Protein: 14.5 Grams Fat: 4.2 Grams Carbs: 45 Grams

Chicken & Mushroom Stew

Preparation Time: 20 minutes

Cooking Time: 20 minutes

Servings: 4

Ingredients:

4 Cloves Garlic, Diced

2 Bay Leaves

7 Ounces White Button Mushrooms

1 ¾ lb. Chicken Breasts, Diced

1 Teaspoon Flavored vinegar

1 Brown Onion, Halved & Sliced

2 Tablespoons Olive Oil

¼ Teaspoon Ground Nutmeg

½ Teaspoon Black Pepper

1 Teaspoon Dijon Mustard

½ Cup Chicken Stock

1/3 Cup Sour Cream

1 Teaspoon Arrowroot Powder

3 Tablespoons Parsley, Fresh & Chopped

Directions:

Press sauté and add the oil. Once the oil is hot add the vinegar and onion, cooking for four minutes.

Add in the mushroom, bay leaves, chicken, nutmeg, garlic, stock cube, pepper, water and mustard. Stir well.

Seal the lid and cook on high pressure for one minute.

Use a natural pressure release for ten minutes and then finish with a quick release.

Take out a few tablespoons of liquid and mix it with the arrowroot powder, pour it in and allow it to thicken for three minutes.

Add in the sour cream, and stir well. Serve warm and garnished with parsley.

Nutrition:

Calories: 249

Protein: 18 Grams

Fat: 17 Grams

Carbs: 5 Grams

Chapter 9: Side Dish Recipes

Apple & Barley Side

Preparation Time: 15 minutes

Cooking Time: 15 minutes

Servings: 4

Ingredients:

1 Cup Barley

2 Cups Water

1 Cup Pesto, Salt Free

1 Green Apple, Chopped

¼ Cup Celery, Chopped

Black Pepper to Taste

Directions:

Put the water, salt, pepper and barely in your instant pot, and then seal the lid. Cook on high pressure for twenty minutes before using a quick release and draining it. Add your apple, pesto, pepper and celery to the barley, and then toss. Serve warm.

Nutrition:

Calories: 200 Protein: 7 Grams Fat: 5 Grams Carbs: 14 Grams

Spinach Dip

Preparation Time: 10 minutes

Cooking Time: 10 minutes

Servings: 4

Ingredients:

1 Bunch Spinach Leaves, Torn

1 Scallion, Sliced

2 Tablespoons Mint Leaves, Chopped

¾ Cup Coconut Cream

Black Pepper to Taste

Directions:

Mix the scallion, mint, cream, spinach and black pepper together. toss well, and seal the lid.

Cook on high pressure for ten minutes, and then use a quick release.

Use an immersion blender to blend before serving.

Nutrition:

Calories: 200

Protein: 8 Grams

Fat: 3 Grams Carbs: 16 Grams

Rice & Endives

Preparation Time: 10 minutes

Cooking Time: 25 minutes

Servings: 4

Ingredients:

1 Tablespoon Olive Oil - 2 Scallions, Chopped

1 Tablespoon Ginger, Grated

3 Cloves Garlic, Minced

1 Teaspoon Chili Sauce

Black Pepper to Taste

1 Cup White Rice - 2 Cups Vegetable Stock

3 Endives, Trimmed & Chopped

Directions: Press sauté and add the oil. Once it's hot add in the ginger, scallions, chili sauce and garlic. Stir while cooking for five minutes. Add the rice and stock, and stir again. Cover, and cook on high pressure for seventeen minutes. Add the endives and pepper, and stir well. Seal the lid and cook on high pressure for five minutes before using a quick release and serve warm.

Nutrition:

Calories: 200 Protein: 8 Grams Fat: 5 Grams Carbs: 16 Grams

Lentils & Peas

Preparation Time: 10 minutes

Cooking Time: 12 minutes

Servings: 6

Ingredients:

½ Cup Red Lentils

1 Tomato, Chopped

½ Cup Yellow Split Peas

1 ½ Cups Water

3 Cloves, Minced

1 Yellow Onion, Chopped

1 Teaspoon Cumin Seeds

1 Teaspoon Ginger, Grated

½ Teaspoon Turmeric Powder

Directions:

Mix your lentils, peas, tomato, water, garlic, onion, cumin, ginger, and turmeric. Stir well, and then seal the lid. Cook on high pressure for twelve minutes, and then sue a quick release. Serve warm.

Nutrition:

Calories: 202 Protein: 5 Grams Fat: 4 Grams Carbs: 14 Grams

Leeks & Fennel

Preparation Time: 10 minutes

Cooking Time: 15 minutes

Servings: 2

Ingredients:

1 Fennel Bulb, Chopped

½ Cup Vegetable Stock, Low Sodium

1 Tablespoon Olive Oil

1 Leek, Chopped

Black Pepper to Taste

Directions:

Mix your fennel, leek, oi, stock and pepper. Seal the lid and cook on high pressure for fifteen minutes.

Use a quick release and serve warm.

Nutrition:

Calories: 162

Protein: 7 Grams

Fat: 5 Grams

Carbs: 7 Grams

Summer Squash Ribbons with Lemon and Ricotta

Preparation Time: 20 minutes

Cooking Time: 0 minutes

Servings: 4

Ingredients:

2 medium zucchini or yellow squash

½ cup ricotta cheese

2 tablespoons fresh mint, chopped, plus additional mint leaves for garnish

2 tablespoons fresh parsley, chopped

Zest of ½ lemon

2 teaspoons lemon juice

½ teaspoon kosher salt

¼ teaspoon freshly ground black pepper

1 tablespoon extra-virgin olive oil

Directions:

Using a vegetable peeler, make ribbons by peeling the summer squash lengthwise. The squash ribbons will resemble the wide pasta, pappardelle.

In a medium bowl, combine the ricotta cheese, mint, parsley, lemon zest, lemon juice, salt, and black pepper.

Place mounds of the squash ribbons evenly on 4 plates then dollop the ricotta mixture on top. Drizzle with the olive oil and garnish with the mint leaves.

Nutrition:

Calories: 90

Total Fat: 6g

Saturated Fat: 2g

Cholesterol: 10mg

Sodium: 180mg

Potassium: 315mg

Total Carbohydrates: 5g

Fiber: 1g

Sugars: 3g

Protein: 5g

Magnesium: 25mg

Calcium: 105mg

Sautéed Kale with Tomato and Garlic

Preparation Time: 5 minutes

Cooking Time: 10 minutes

Servings: 4

Ingredients: 1 tablespoon extra-virgin olive oil

4 garlic cloves, sliced

¼ teaspoon red pepper flakes

2 bunches kale, stemmed and chopped or torn into pieces

1 (14.5-ounce) can no-salt-added diced tomatoes

½ teaspoon kosher salt

Directions: Heat the olive oil in a wok or large skillet over medium-high heat. Add the garlic and red pepper flakes, and sauté until fragrant, about 30 seconds. Add the kale and sauté, about 3 to 5 minutes, until the kale shrinks down a bit. Add the tomatoes and the salt, stir together, and cook for 3 to 5 minutes, or until the liquid reduces and the kale cooks down further and becomes tender.

Nutrition: Calories: 110 Total Fat: 5g

Saturated Fat: 1g Cholesterol: 0mg Sodium: 222mg

Potassium: 535mg Total Carbohydrates: 15g Fiber: 6g

Sugars: 6g Protein: 6g Magnesium: 50mg Calcium: 182mg

Roasted Broccoli with Tahini Yogurt Sauce

Preparation Time: 15 minutes

Cooking Time: 30 minutes

Servings: 4

Ingredients:

1½ to 2 pounds broccoli, stalk trimmed and cut into slices, head cut into florets

1 lemon, sliced into ¼-inch-thick rounds

3 tablespoons extra-virgin olive oil

½ teaspoon kosher salt

¼ teaspoon freshly ground black pepper

½ cup plain Greek yogurt

2 tablespoons tahini

1 tablespoon lemon juice

¼ teaspoon kosher salt

1 teaspoon sesame seeds, for garnish (optional)

Directions:

Preheat the oven to 425°F. Line a baking sheet with parchment paper or foil.

In a large bowl, gently toss the broccoli, lemon slices, olive oil, salt, and black pepper to combine. Arrange the broccoli in a single layer on the prepared baking sheet. Roast 15 minutes, stir, and roast another 15 minutes, until golden brown.

TO MAKE THE TAHINI YOGURT SAUCE

In a medium bowl, combine the yogurt, tahini, lemon juice, and salt; mix well.

Spread the tahini yogurt sauce on a platter or large plate and top with the broccoli and lemon slices. Garnish with the sesame seeds (if desired).

Nutrition:

Calories: 245

Total Fat: 16g

Saturated Fat: 2g

Cholesterol: 2mg

Sodium: 305mg

Potassium: 835mg

Total Carbohydrates: 20g

Fiber: 7g

Sugars: 6g

Protein: 12g Magnesium: 65mg Calcium: 185mg

Green Beans with Pine Nuts and Garlic

Preparation Time: 10 minutes

Cooking Time: 20 minutes

Servings: 4-6

Ingredients:

1 pound green beans, trimmed

1 head garlic (10 to 12 cloves), smashed

2 tablespoons extra-virgin olive oil - ½ teaspoon kosher salt

¼ teaspoon red pepper flakes - 1 tablespoon white wine vinegar

¼ cup pine nuts, toasted

Directions: Preheat the oven to 425°F. Line a baking sheet with parchment paper or foil. In a large bowl, combine the green beans, garlic, olive oil, salt, and red pepper flakes and mix together. Arrange in a single layer on the baking sheet. Roast for 10 minutes, stir, and roast for another 10 minutes, or until golden brown. Mix the cooked green beans with the vinegar and top with the pine nuts.

Nutrition:

Calories: 165 Total Fat: 13g Saturated Fat: 1g Cholesterol: 0mg

Sodium: 150mg Potassium: 325mg Total Carbohydrates: 12g Fiber: 4g

Sugars: 4g Protein: 4g Magnesium: 52mg Calcium: 60mg

Roasted Harissa Carrots

Preparation Time: 10 minutes

Cooking Time: 15 minutes

Servings: 4

Ingredients:

1 pound carrots, peeled and sliced into 1-inch-thick rounds

2 tablespoons extra-virgin olive oil

2 tablespoons harissa

1 teaspoon honey

1 teaspoon ground cumin

½ teaspoon kosher salt

½ cup fresh parsley, chopped

Directions:

Preheat the oven to 450°F. Line a baking sheet with parchment paper or foil. In a large bowl, combine the carrots, olive oil, harissa, honey, cumin, and salt. Arrange in a single layer on the baking sheet. Roast for 15 minutes. Remove from the oven, add the parsley, and toss together.

Nutrition: Calories: 120 Total Fat: 8g Saturated Fat: 1gCholesterol: 0mg

Sodium: 255mg Potassium: 415mg Total Carbohydrates: 13g Fiber: 4g

Sugars: 7g Protein: 1g Magnesium: 18mg Calcium: 53mg

Cucumbers with Feta, Mint, and Sumac

Preparation Time: 15 minutes

Cooking Time: 0 minutes

Servings: 4

Ingredients:

1 tablespoon extra-virgin olive oil

1 tablespoon lemon juice

2 teaspoons ground sumac

½ teaspoon kosher salt

2 hothouse or English cucumbers, diced

¼ cup crumbled feta cheese

1 tablespoon fresh mint, chopped

1 tablespoon fresh parsley, chopped - ⅛ teaspoon red pepper flakes

Directions: In a large bowl, whisk together the olive oil, lemon juice, sumac, and salt. Add the cucumber and feta cheese and toss well. Transfer to a serving dish and sprinkle with the mint, parsley, and red pepper flakes.

Nutrition: Calories: 85 Total Fat: 6g Saturated Fat: 2g Cholesterol: 8mg

Sodium: 230mg Potassium: 295mg Total Carbohydrates: 8g Fiber: 1g

Sugars: 4g Protein: 3g Magnesium: 27mg Calcium: 80mg

Cherry Tomato Bruschetta

Preparation Time: 15 minutes

Cooking Time: 0 minutes

Servings: 4

Ingredients:

8 ounces assorted cherry tomatoes, halved

⅓ cup fresh herbs, chopped (such as basil, parsley, tarragon, dill)

1 tablespoon extra-virgin olive oil

¼ teaspoon kosher salt

⅛ teaspoon freshly ground black pepper

¼ cup ricotta cheese

4 slices whole-wheat bread, toasted

Directions:

Combine the tomatoes, herbs, olive oil, salt, and black pepper in a medium bowl and mix gently. Spread 1 tablespoon of ricotta cheese onto each slice of toast. Spoon one-quarter of the tomato mixture onto each bruschetta. If desired, garnish with more herbs.

Nutrition: Calories: 100 Total Fat: 6g Saturated Fat: 1g Cholesterol: 5mg

Sodium: 135mg Potassium: 210mg Total Carbohydrates: 10g

Fiber: 2g Sugars: 2g Protein: 4g Magnesium: 22mg Calcium: 60mg

Roasted Red Pepper Hummus

Preparation Time: 15 minutes

Cooking Time: 0 minutes

Servings: 2 cups

Ingredients:

1 (15-ounce) can low-sodium chickpeas, drained and rinsed

3 ounces jarred roasted red bell peppers, drained

3 tablespoons tahini

3 tablespoons lemon juice

1 garlic clove, peeled

¾ teaspoon kosher salt

¼ teaspoon freshly ground black pepper

3 tablespoons extra-virgin olive oil

¼ teaspoon cayenne pepper (optional)

Fresh herbs, chopped, for garnish (optional)

Directions:

In a food processor, add the chickpeas, red bell peppers, tahini, lemon juice, garlic, salt, and black pepper. Pulse 5 to 7 times. Add the olive oil and process until smooth. Add the cayenne pepper and garnish with chopped herbs, if desired.

Nutrition:

Calories: 130

Total Fat: 8g

Saturated Fat: 1g

Cholesterol: 0mg

Sodium: 150mg

Potassium: 125mg

Total Carbohydrates: 11g

Fiber: 2g

Sugars: 1g

Protein: 4g

Magnesium: 20mg

Calcium: 48mg

Baked Eggplant Baba Ganoush

Preparation Time: 10 minutes

Cooking Time: 1 hour

Servings: 4

Ingredients:

2 pounds (about 2 medium to large) eggplant

3 tablespoons tahini

Zest of 1 lemon

2 tablespoons lemon juice

¾ teaspoon kosher salt

½ teaspoon ground sumac, plus more for sprinkling (optional)

⅓ cup fresh parsley, chopped

1 tablespoon extra-virgin olive oil

Directions:

Preheat the oven to 350°F. Place the eggplants directly on the rack and bake for 60 minutes, or until the skin is wrinkly.

In a food processor add the tahini, lemon zest, lemon juice, salt, and sumac. Carefully cut open the baked eggplant and scoop the flesh into the food processor. Process until the ingredients are well blended.

Place in a serving dish and mix in the parsley. Drizzle with the olive oil and sprinkle with sumac, if desired.

Nutrition:

Calories: 50

Total Fat: 4g

Saturated Fat: 1g

Cholesterol: 0mg

Sodium: 110mg

Potassium: 42mg

Total Carbohydrates: 2g

Fiber: 1g

Sugars: 0g

Protein: 1g

Magnesium: 7mg

Calcium: 28mg

White Bean Romesco Dip

Preparation Time: 10 minutes

Cooking Time: 0 minutes

Servings: 4

Ingredients:

2 red bell peppers, or 1 (12-ounce) jar roasted sweet red peppers in water, drained

2 garlic cloves, peeled

½ cup roasted unsalted almonds

1 6-inch multigrain pita, torn into small pieces

1 teaspoon red pepper flakes

1 (14.5-ounce) can no-salt-added diced tomatoes

1 (14.5-ounce) can low-sodium cannellini beans, drained and rinsed

1 tablespoon fresh parsley, chopped

1 teaspoon sweet or smoked paprika

1 teaspoon kosher salt

¼ teaspoon black pepper

¼ cup extra-virgin olive oil

2 tablespoons red wine vinegar

2 teaspoons lemon juice (optional)

Directions:

If you are using raw peppers, roast them following the steps (see *Tip*), then roughly chop. If using jarred roasted peppers, proceed to step 2.

In a food processor, add the garlic and pulse until finely minced. Scrape down the sides of the bowl and add the almonds, pita, and red pepper flakes, and process until minced. Scrape down the sides of the bowl and add the bell peppers, tomatoes, beans, parsley, paprika, salt, and black pepper. Process until smooth.

With the food processor running, add the olive oil and vinegar, and process until smooth. Taste, and add the lemon juice to brighten, if desired.

Nutrition:

Calories: 180

Total Fat: 10g

Saturated Fat: 1g

Cholesterol: 0mg

Sodium: 285mg

Potassium: 270mg Total Carbohydrates: 20g Fiber: 4g

Sugars: 3g Protein: 6g Magnesium: 40mg Calcium: 65mg

Roasted Cherry Tomato Caprese

Preparation Time: 15 minutes

Cooking Time: 30 minutes

Servings: 4

Ingredients:

2 pints (about 20 ounces) cherry tomatoes

6 thyme sprigs

6 garlic cloves, smashed

2 tablespoons extra-virgin olive oil

½ teaspoon kosher salt

8 ounces fresh, unsalted mozzarella, cut into bite-size slices

¼ cup basil, chopped or cut into ribbons

Loaf of crusty whole-wheat bread for serving

Directions:

Preheat the oven to 350°F. Line a baking sheet with parchment paper or foil.

Put the tomatoes, thyme, garlic, olive oil, and salt into a large bowl and mix together. Place on the prepared baking sheet in a single layer. Roast for 30 minutes, or until the tomatoes are bursting and juicy.

Place the mozzarella on a platter or in a bowl. Pour all the tomato mixture, including the juices, over the mozzarella. Garnish with the basil.

Serve with crusty bread.

Nutrition:

Calories: 250

Total Fat: 17g

Saturated Fat: 7g

Cholesterol: 31mg

Sodium: 157mg

Potassium: 425mg

Total Carbohydrates: 9g

Fiber: 2g

Sugars: 4g

Protein: 17g

Magnesium: 35mg

Calcium: 445mg

Italian Crepe with Herbs and Onion

Preparation Time: 15 minutes

Cooking Time: 20 minutes per crepe

Servings: 6

Ingredients:

2 cups cold water

1 cup chickpea flour

½ teaspoon kosher salt

¼ teaspoon freshly ground black pepper

3½ tablespoons extra-virgin olive oil, divided

½ onion, julienned

½ cup fresh herbs, chopped (thyme, sage, and rosemary are all nice on their own or as a mix)

Directions:

In a large bowl, whisk together the water, flour, salt, and black pepper. Add 2 tablespoons of the olive oil and whisk. Let the batter sit at room temperature for at least 30 minutes.

Preheat the oven to 450°F. Place a 12-inch cast-iron pan or oven-safe skillet in the oven to warm as the oven comes to temperature.

Remove the hot pan from the oven carefully, add ½ tablespoon of the olive oil and one-third of the onion, stir, and place the pan back in the oven. Cook, stirring occasionally, until the onions are golden brown, 5 to 8 minutes.

Remove the pan from the oven and pour in one-third of the batter (about 1 cup), sprinkle with one-third of the herbs, and put it back in the oven. Bake for 10 minutes, or until firm and the edges are set.

Increase the oven setting to broil and cook 3 to 5 minutes, or until golden brown. Slide the crepe onto the cutting board and repeat twice more. Halve the crepes and cut into wedges. Serve warm or at room temperature.

Nutrition:

Calories: 135

Total Fat: 9g

Saturated Fat: 1g

Cholesterol: 0mg

Sodium: 105mg

Potassium: 165mg

Total Carbohydrates: 11g Fiber: 2g

Sugars: 2g Protein: 4g Magnesium: 30mg Calcium: 20mg

Pita Pizza with Olives, Feta, and Red Onion

Preparation Time: 15 minutes

Cooking Time: 10 minutes

Servings: 4

Ingredients:

4 (6-inch) whole-wheat pitas

1 tablespoon extra-virgin olive oil

½ cup hummus (store-bought or *Roasted Red Pepper Hummus*)

½ bell pepper, julienned

½ red onion, julienned

¼ cup olives, pitted and chopped

¼ cup crumbled feta cheese

¼ teaspoon red pepper flakes

¼ cup fresh herbs, chopped (mint, parsley, oregano, or a mix)

Directions:

Preheat the broiler to low. Line a baking sheet with parchment paper or foil.

Place the pitas on the prepared baking sheet and brush both sides with the olive oil. Broil 1 to 2 minutes per side until starting to turn golden brown.

Spread 2 tablespoons hummus on each pita. Top the pitas with bell pepper, onion, olives, feta cheese, and red pepper flakes. Broil again until the cheese softens and starts to get golden brown, 4 to 6 minutes, being careful not to burn the pitas.

Remove from broiler and top with the herbs.

Nutrition:

Calories: 185

Total Fat: 11g

Saturated Fat: 2g

Cholesterol: 8mg

Sodium: 285mg

Potassium: 13mg

Total Carbohydrates: 17g

Fiber: 3g

Sugars: 3g

Protein: 5g

Magnesium: 18mg

Calcium: 91mg

Roasted Za'atar Chickpeas

Preparation Time: 5 minutes

Cooking Time: 1 hour

Servings: 8

Ingredients:

3 tablespoons za'atar

2 tablespoons extra-virgin olive oil

½ teaspoon kosher salt

¼ teaspoon freshly ground black pepper

4 cups cooked chickpeas, or 2 (15-ounce) cans, drained and rinsed

Directions: Preheat the oven to 400°F. Line a baking sheet with foil or parchment paper. In a large bowl, combine the za'atar, olive oil, salt, and black pepper. Add the chickpeas and mix thoroughly. Spread the chickpeas in a single layer on the prepared baking sheet. Bake for 45 to 60 minutes, or until golden brown and crispy. Cool and store in an airtight container at room temperature for up to 1 week.

Nutrition: Calories: 150

Total Fat: 6g Saturated Fat: 1g Cholesterol: 0mg Sodium: 230mg

Potassium: 182mg Total Carbohydrates: 17g; Fiber 6g Sugars: 3g

Protein: 6g Magnesium: 32mg Calcium: 52mg

Roasted Rosemary Olives

Preparation Time: 5 minutes

Cooking Time: 25 minutes

Servings: 4

Ingredients:

1 cup mixed variety olives, pitted and rinsed

2 tablespoons lemon juice

1 tablespoon extra-virgin olive oil

6 garlic cloves, peeled

4 rosemary sprigs

Directions:

Preheat the oven to 400°F. Line the baking sheet with parchment paper or foil. Combine the olives, lemon juice, olive oil, and garlic in a medium bowl and mix together. Spread in a single layer on the prepared baking sheet. Sprinkle on the rosemary. Roast for 25 minutes, tossing halfway through. Remove the rosemary leaves from the stem and place in a serving bowl. Add the olives and mix before serving.

Nutrition: Calories: 100 Total Fat: 9g Saturated Fat: 1g Cholesterol: 0mg

Sodium: 260mg Potassium: 31mg Total Carbohydrates: 4g Fiber: 0g

Sugars: 0g Protein: 0g Magnesium: 3mg Calcium: 11mg

Crispy Cinnamon Apple Chips

Preparation Time: 15 minutes

Cooking Time: 1 hour and 15 minutes

Servings: 4

Ingredients:

3 apples, thinly sliced crosswise, seeded

1 tablespoon ground cinnamon

1 teaspoon granulated sugar

¼ teaspoon kosher salt

Directions:

Preheat the oven to 275°F. Coat a baking sheet with cooking spray. In a large bowl, whisk together the cinnamon, sugar, and salt. Add the apple slices and toss to evenly coat. Line up the apple slices on the baking sheet and roast for 45 minutes, then flip each chip and roast for another 45 minutes, until dried and crispy. Once cooled, store in an airtight container or plastic bag for up to 7 days.

Nutrition:

Total Calories: 80 Total Fat: 0g Saturated Fat: 0g

Cholesterol: 0mg Sodium: 147mg Potassium: 155mg

Total Carbohydrate: 21g Fiber: 4g Sugars: 15g Protein: 0g

Coconut Date Energy Bites

Preparation Time: 10 minutes

Cooking Time: 0 minutes

Servings: 4

Ingredients:

12 pitted Medjool dates

½ cup unsweetened shredded coconut

½ cup chopped walnuts or almonds

1½ tablespoons melted coconut oil

Directions:

Place all the ingredients in a food processor and pulse until the mixture becomes a paste. Form 2-inch bites, place in an airtight container, and store in the refrigerator for up to 2 weeks.

Nutrition:

Total Calories: 110

Total Fat: 6g

Saturated Fat: 3g

Cholesterol: 0mg Sodium: 1mg Potassium: 151mg

Total Carbohydrate: 16g Fiber: 2g Sugars: 13g Protein: 1g

Roasted Root Vegetable Chips with French Onion Yogurt Dip

Preparation Time: 20 minutes

Cooking Time: 20 minutes

Servings: 6

Ingredients:

FOR THE ROASTED ROOT VEGETABLE CHIPS:

1 sweet potato

1 Yukon Gold potato

1 beet

3 tablespoons canola oil

¼ teaspoon kosher salt

FOR THE FRENCH ONION YOGURT DIP:

1 tablespoon canola oil

1 yellow onion, peeled and thinly sliced

3 cloves garlic, peeled and minced

1 cup nonfat plain Greek yogurt

1 tablespoon mayonnaise

1 teaspoon Worcestershire sauce

½ teaspoon ground black pepper

½ teaspoon onion powder - ¼ teaspoon kosher or sea salt

¼ teaspoon dried mustard powder, ⅛ teaspoon ground cayenne pepper

TO MAKE THE ROASTED ROOT VEGETABLE CHIPS:

Directions:

Preheat the oven to 425°F. Coat a large baking sheet with cooking spray.

Thinly slice the sweet potato, Yukon Gold potato, and beet with a mandoline. Be careful! Coat them in the canola oil and sprinkle with the salt. Roast for about 16 minutes, flipping after 8 minutes, until crispy and lightly browned.

TO MAKE THE FRENCH ONION YOGURT DIP:

Heat the canola oil in a skillet over medium-low heat. Add the onion and sauté for 8 to 10 minutes, until caramelized and brown. Stir in the garlic and cook until fragrant, about 1 minute. Transfer the mixture to a bowl and add the Greek yogurt, mayonnaise, Worcestershire sauce, black pepper, onion powder, salt, dried mustard powder, and cayenne pepper. Mix until combined. The chips are best when served immediately. The sauce will keep in the refrigerator for 5 days.

Nutrition: Total Calories: 168 Total Fat: 11g

Saturated Fat: 1g Cholesterol: 2mg Sodium: 266mg Potassium: 342mg

Total Carbohydrate: 13g Fiber: 1g Sugars: 5gProtein: 5g

Stovetop Cheese Popcorn

Preparation Time: 10 minutes

Cooking Time: 0 minutes

Servings: 15

Ingredients:

¼ cup canola oil

½ cup white or yellow popcorn kernels

3 tablespoons nutritional yeast

½ teaspoon kosher salt

Directions:

Heat the canola oil over medium-high heat in a large stockpot. Add the popcorn kernels and place a lid on the pot. Let cook, shaking the pot periodically, until the popping stops. Remove from the heat, transfer to a large bowl, and top with the nutritional yeast and salt, shaking the bowl to coat the hot popcorn.

Nutrition:

Total Calories: 54 Total Fat: 4g

Saturated Fat: 0g Cholesterol: 0mg Sodium: 77mg Potassium: 0mg

Total Carbohydrate: 5g Fiber: 1g Sugars: 0g Protein: 1g

Sweet & Salty Nut Mix

Preparation Time: 10 minutes

Cooking Time: 45 minutes

Servings: 6

Ingredients:

1 tablespoon chili powder

½ tablespoon ground cinnamon

½ tablespoon granulated sugar

1 teaspoon ground ginger

½ teaspoon kosher or sea salt

¼ teaspoon ground cayenne pepper (optional)

2 large egg whites

½ cup unsalted peanuts

½ cup unsalted almonds

¼ cup unsalted cashews

Directions:

Preheat the oven to 300°F. Coat a baking sheet with cooking spray.

In a small bowl, whisk together the chili powder, cinnamon, sugar, ginger, salt, and cayenne pepper, if using.

In a larger bowl, whip the egg whites until slightly frothy. Then, stir in the peanuts, almonds, and cashews. After the peanuts, almonds, and cashews are coated, stir in the spice mixture until combined.

Transfer to the baking sheet and spread them out evenly. Bake for 40 to 45 minutes, until slightly browned.

Once cooled, store in an airtight container or plastic bag for up to 2 to 3 weeks.

Nutrition:

Total Calories: 204

Total Fat: g16

Saturated Fat: 2g

Cholesterol: 0mg

Sodium: 227mg

Potassium: 257mg

Total Carbohydrate: 11g

Fiber: 3g

Sugars: 3g

Protein: 8g

Chapter 10: Dessert Recipes

Easy Cinnamon Baked Apples

Preparation Time: 5 minutes

Cooking Time: 45 minutes

Servings: 4

Ingredients:

4 apples, cored, peeled, and sliced thin

½ tablespoon ground cinnamon

¼ cup brown sugar

¼ teaspoon ground nutmeg

Optional: 2 teaspoons freshly squeezed lemon juice

Directions:

Preheat the oven to 375°F. Place apples in a mixing bowl and gently mix all the other ingredients together. Put apples in a nonstick pan. Cover and place in the oven. Bake for 45 minutes, stirring at least once every 15 minutes. Once they are soft, cook for another few minutes to thicken the cinnamon sauce. Serve.

Nutrition: Total Calories: 117 Total Fat: 1g Saturated Fat: 0g

Cholesterol: 0mg Sodium: 4mg Potassium: 206mg

Total Carbohydrate: 34g Fiber: 5g Sugars: 28g Protein: 0g

Chocolate Cake In a Mug

Preparation Time: 5 minutes

Cooking Time: 1 minutes

Servings: 1

Ingredients:

3 tablespoons white whole-wheat flour

2 tablespoons unsweetened cocoa powder

2 teaspoons sugar

⅛ teaspoon baking powder

1 egg white - ½ teaspoon olive oil

3 tablespoons nonfat or low-fat milk -½ teaspoon vanilla extract

Cooking spray

Directions: Place the flour, cocoa, sugar, and baking powder in a small bowl and whisk until combined. Then add in the egg white, olive oil, milk, and vanilla extract, and mix to combine. Spray a mug with cooking spray and pour batter into mug. Microwave on high for 60 seconds or until set. Serve.

Nutrition: Total Calories: 217 Total Fat: 4g

Saturated Fat: 1g Cholesterol: 1mg Sodium: 139mg Potassium: 244mg

Total Carbohydrate: 35g Fiber: 7g Sugars: 12g Protein: 11g

Peanut Butter Banana "Ice Cream"

Preparation Time: 10 minutes

Cooking Time: 0 minutes

Servings: 4

Ingredients:

4 bananas, very ripe, peeled and sliced into ½-inch rings

2 tablespoons peanut butter

Directions:

On a large baking sheet or plate, spread the banana slices in an even layer. Freeze for 1 to 2 hours.

In a food processor or blender, puree the frozen banana until it forms a smooth and creamy mixture, scraping down the bowl as needed. Add the peanut butter, pureeing until just combined. For a soft-serve ice cream consistency, serve immediately. For a harder consistency, place the ice cream in the freezer for a few hours before serving.

Nutrition:

Total Calories: 153

Total Fat: 4g

Saturated Fat: 1g Cholesterol: 0mg Sodium: 4mg Potassium: 422mg

Total Carbohydrate: 29g Fiber: 4g Sugars: 15g Protein: 3g

Banana-Cashew Cream Mousse

Preparation Time: 55 minutes

Cooking Time: 0 minutes

Servings: 2

Ingredients:

½ cup cashews, presoaked

1 tablespoon honey

1 teaspoon vanilla extract

1 large banana, sliced (reserve 4 slices for garnish)

1 cup plain nonfat Greek yogurt

Directions:

Place the cashews in a small bowl and cover with 1 cup of water. Soak at room temperature for 2 to 3 hours. Drain, rinse, and set aside. Place honey, vanilla extract, cashews, and bananas in a blender or food processor. Blend until smooth. Place mixture in a medium bowl. Fold in yogurt, mix well. Cover. Chill in refrigerator, covered, for at least 45 minutes. Portion mousse into 2 serving bowls. Garnish each with 2 banana slices.

Nutrition: Total Calories: 329 Total Fat: 14g

Saturated Fat: 3g Cholesterol: 8mg Sodium: 64mg Potassium: 507mg

Total Carbohydrate: 37g Fiber: 3g Sugars: 24g Protein: 17g

Peach and Blueberry Tart

Preparation Time: 10 minutes

Cooking Time: 30 minutes

Servings: 6-8

Ingredients:

1 sheet frozen puff pastry

1 cup fresh blueberries

4 peaches, pitted and sliced

3 tablespoons sugar

2 tablespoons cornstarch

1 tablespoon freshly squeezed lemon juice

Cooking spray

1 tablespoon nonfat or low-fat milk

Confectioners' sugar, for dusting

Directions:

Thaw puff pastry at room temperature for at least 30 minutes.

Preheat the oven to 400°F.

In a large bowl, toss the blueberries, peaches, sugar, cornstarch, and lemon juice.

Spray a round pie pan with cooking spray.

Unfold pastry and place on prepared pie pan.

Arrange the peach slices so they are slightly overlapping. Spread the blueberries on top of the peaches.

Drape pastry over the outside of the fruit and press pleats firmly together. Brush with milk.

Bake in the bottom third of the oven until crust is golden, about 30 minutes.

Cool on a rack.

Sprinkle pastry with confectioners' sugar. Serve.

Nutrition:

Total Calories: 119

Total Fat: 3g

Saturated Fat: 1g

Cholesterol: 0mg

Sodium: 21mg

Potassium: 155mg

Total Carbohydrate: 23g Fiber: 2g Sugars: 15gProtein: 1g

Sriracha Parsnip Fries

Preparation Time: 10 minutes

Cooking Time: 25 minutes

Servings: 4

Ingredients:

1 pound parsnips, peeled, cut into 3 × ½-inch strips

1 tablespoon olive oil

1 teaspoon dried rosemary

Sriracha to taste

Salt and pepper to taste

Directions:

Preheat oven to 450°F. Mix parsnips, rosemary, and oil in a medium size bowl. Season with salt, pepper, and sriracha to taste and toss to coat. Lay parsnips on a baking sheet making sure the strips don't overlap. (If they are touching they will become mushy instead of crispy.) Bake for 10 minutes. Turn and roast until parsnips are browned in spots, 10 to 15 minutes longer. If you want them to be extra crispy, turn the broiler on for the last 2 to 3 minutes. Remove from oven and enjoy.

Nutrition: Total Calories: 112 Total Fat: 4g Saturated Fat: 1g

Cholesterol: 0mg Sodium: 12mg Potassium: 419mg

Total Carbohydrate: 20g Fiber: 4g Sugars: 5g Protein: 2g

Tortilla Strawberry Chips

Preparation Time: 10 minutes

Cooking Time: 25 minutes

Servings: 6

Ingredients:

15 strawberry

¼ tsp. cayenne

2 tbsps. organic extra virgin olive oil

12 whole wheat grain tortillas

1 tbsp. chili powder

Directions:

Spread the tortillas for the lined baking sheet, add the oil, chili powder, strawberry and cayenne, toss, introduce inside oven and bake at 350 0F for 25 minutes.

Divide into bowls and serve as a side dish.

Enjoy!

Nutrition: Calories: 199 Fat: 3 g

Carbs: 12 g Protein: 5 g Sugars: 7 g Sodium: 9.8 mg

Almond Rice Pudding

Preparation Time: 10 minutes

Cooking Time: 30 minutes

Servings: 3-4

Ingredients:

¼ c. sugar

1 tsp. vanilla

3 c. milk

1 c. white rice

¼ c. toasted almonds

Cinnamon

¼ tsp. almond extract

Directions:

Get the milk and rice together in a pan and boil and simmer it by lowering the heat for half an hour with the top on till the rice softens up a bit.

Take it off the burner and put in sugar, almond, vanilla and cinnamon.

Garish roasted almonds at the top and eat it warm.

Nutrition: Calories: 80 Fat: 1.5 g

Carbs: 16 g Protein: 1 g Sugars: 7 g Sodium: 121.4 mg

Sweet Potatoes and Apples Mix

Preparation Time: 10 minutes

Cooking Time: 1 hour and 10 minutes

Servings: 1

Ingredients:

1 tbsp. low-fat butter

½ lb. cored and chopped apples

2 tbsps. water

2 lbs. sweet potatoes

Directions:

Arrange the potatoes around the lined baking sheet, bake inside oven at 400 0F for an hour, peel them and mash them in the meat processor.

Put apples in the very pot, add the river, bring using a boil over medium heat, reduce temperature, and cook for ten minutes.

Transfer to your bowl, add mashed potatoes, stir well and serve every day.

Enjoy!

Nutrition: Calories: 140

Fat: 1 g Carbs: 8 g Protein: 6 g Sugars: 2.6 g Sodium: 493.3 mg

Sautéed Bananas with Orange Sauce

Preparation Time: 5 minutes

Cooking Time: 5 minutes

Servings: 4

Ingredients:

¼ c. frozen pure orange juice concentrate

2 tbsps. margarine

¼ c. sliced almonds

1 tsp. orange zest

1 tsp. fresh grated ginger

4 firm, sliced ripe bananas

1 tsp. cinnamon

Directions: Melt the margarine over medium heat in a large skillet, until it bubbles but before it begins to brown.   Add the cinnamon, ginger, and orange zest. Cook, while stirring, for 1 minute before adding the orange juice concentrate. Cook, while stirring until an even sauce has formed.   Add the bananas and cook, stirring carefully for 1-2 minutes, or until warmed and evenly coated with the sauce.   Serve warm with sliced almonds.

Nutrition: Calories: 164.3

Fat: 9.0 gCarbs: 21.4 g Protein: 2.3 g Sugars: 26 g Sodium: 100 mg

Caramelized Blood Oranges with Ginger Cream

Preparation Time: 10 minutes

Cooking Time: 15 minutes

Servings: 4

Ingredients:

2 tbsps. low sugar orange marmalade

1 tbsp. divided fresh grated ginger

4 c. peeled and sliced blood oranges

2 tbsps. brown sugar

Candied orange peel

½ c. coconut cream

Directions:

Begin by preheating the broiler.

In a small saucepan combine the orange marmalade and two teaspoons of the fresh ginger. Heat over low heat and stir until the mixture becomes slightly liquefied.

Place a thin layer of the oranges into the bottom of four large baking ramekins and then brush with the marmalade mixture. Repeat this step until all of the oranges have been used. Pour any remaining gingered marmalade over the tops of the ramekins.

Sprinkle each ramekin with brown sugar and place under the broiler for approximately 5 minutes, or until caramelized.

Serve warm garnished with coconut cream and candied orange peel, if desired.

To make the coconut cream: Take one can of pure, unsweetened coconut milk and place it in your refrigerator for 24 hours. Take the can out of the refrigerator and scoop out the thick cream that has settled on top. Place this in a bowl, along with one teaspoon of ginger and beat until creamy.

Nutrition:

Calories: 220.2

Fat: 10.7 g

Carbs: 32.4 g

Protein: 2.4 g

Sugars: 19.5 g

Sodium: 143.7 mg

Grilled Minted Watermelon

Preparation Time: 10 minutes

Cooking Time: 10 minutes

Servings: 4

Ingredients:

1 tbsp. honey

¼ c. finely chopped fresh mint

8 thick deseeded watermelon slices

Directions:

Prepare and preheat a stovetop grill.

Lightly press towels against the watermelon slices to remove as much excess moisture as possible.

Lightly brush both sides of the watermelon slices with honey.

Place the watermelon slices on the grill and grill for approximately 3 minutes per side, or until slightly caramelized.

Serve warm, sprinkled with fresh mint.

Nutrition:

Calories: 199.2.

Fat: 2.6 g Carbs: 45.7 g Protein: 3.8 g Sugars: 10.4 g Sodium: 219.8 mg

Caramelized Apricot Pots

Preparation Time: 10 minutes

Cooking Time: 5 minutes

Servings: 6

Ingredients:

¼ c. white sugar

2 tsps. lemon juice

½ tsp. thyme

3 c. sliced apricots

1 tbsp. brown sugar

1 c. part skim ricotta cheese

1 tsp. lemon zest

Directions:

Preheat the broiler of your oven.

Place the apricots in a bowl and toss with the lemon juice.

In another bowl, combine the ricotta cheese, thyme, and lemon zest. Mix well.

Spread a layer of the ricotta mixture into the bottoms of 6 large baking ramekins.

Spoon the apricots over the top of the ricotta cheese in each.

Combine the white sugar and brown sugar. Sprinkle evenly over the apricots, avoiding large clumps of sugar as much as possible.

Place the ramekins under the broiler for approximately 5 minutes, or until caramelized.

Serve warm.

Nutrition:

Calories: 133.6

Fat: 3.6 g

Carbs: 21.6 g

Protein: 5.8 g

Sugars: 6 g

Sodium: 206 mg

Melon Mojito Granita

Preparation Time: 10 minutes

Cooking Time: 0 minutes

Servings: 6

Ingredients:

¼ c. chopped fresh mint

¼ c. lime juice

4 c. cubed cantaloupe melon

1 c. peach nectar

Directions:

Combine the melon, peach nectar, lime juice, and mint in a blender or food processor. Blend until smooth.

Place the mixture in a shallow metal pan and place in the freezer.

Check the mixture every 30 minutes or so. Using a spoon or fork, mix and scrape the mixture at every check, until a slushy ice has formed. This will take a couple of hours.

Take out of the freezer and let soften slightly before serving.

Serve with fresh fruit, if desired.

Nutrition: Calories: 55.7 Fat: 0 g Carbs: 13.8 g Protein: 0.8 g Sugars: 12.5 g Sodium: 3 mg

Mocha Pops

Preparation Time: 10 minutes

Cooking Time: 0 minutes

Servings: 4-6

Ingredients:

½ tsp. pure vanilla extract

2 tbsps. honey

½ c. chopped almonds

¼ c. cooled brewed espresso

2 c. coconut milk

2 tbsps. dark cocoa powder

Directions:

In a blender, combine the coconut milk, honey, cocoa powder, espresso, and vanilla extract. Blend until creamy.

Pour the mixture into freeze pop molds and sprinkle with almonds.

Place in the freezer and freeze for at least 4 hours before enjoying.

Nutrition:

Calories: 317.3

Fat: 27.3 g Carbs: 17.3 g Protein: 4.6 g Sugars: 5 g Sodium: 26 mg

Rhubarb Pie

Preparation Time: 10 minutes

Cooking Time: 20 minutes

Servings: 12

Ingredients:

4 c. chopped rhubarb

8 oz. low-fat cream cheese

1 c. melted low-fat butter

1 ¼ c. coconut sugar

2 c. whole wheat flour

1 c. chopped pecans

1 c. sliced strawberries

Directions: In a bowl, combine the flour while using the butter, pecans and ¼ cup sugar and stir well. Transfer this for some pie pan, press well in for the pan, introduce inside the oven and bake at 350 0F for 20 minutes. In a pan, combine the strawberries with all the current rhubarb, cream cheese and 1 cup sugar, stir well and cook over medium heat for 4 minutes. Spread this inside the pie crust whilst inside fridge for the couple hours before slicing and serving. Enjoy!

Nutrition: Calories: 162

Fat: 5 g Carbs: 15 g Protein: 6 g Sugars: 16.6 g Sodium: 411 mg

Berry No Bake Bars

Preparation Time: 10 minutes

Cooking Time: 0 minutes

Servings: 18

Ingredients:

1 c. natural peanut butter

¼ c. chopped dried blueberries

3 c. oatmeal

¼ c. chopped dried cranberries

3 tbsps. honey

Directions:

Line a baking pan with wax paper or parchment paper.

Microwave the peanut butter for 10-15 seconds, just until it softens and begins to liquefy. Combine the oatmeal, peanut butter, honey, cranberries, and blueberries together in a bowl and mix until blended. Spread the mixture out evenly into the pan. Place in the refrigerator and let set for 2 hours before cutting into squares.

Nutrition: Calories: 145.0 Fat: 6.4 g Carbs: 17.9 g Protein: 4.4 g Sugars: 17.9 g Sodium: 102.4 mg

Tropical Fruit Napoleon

Preparation Time: 20 minutes

Cooking Time: 0 minutes

Servings: 6-8

Ingredients:

1 tbsp. finely chopped fresh lemongrass

1 c. cubed mango

1 tsp. vanilla extract

1 peeled and cored whole pineapple

1 c. shredded unsweetened coconut

2 c. cubed papaya

2 c. light whipping cream

Directions:

Add the vanilla extract to the whipping cream and beat until thick and creamy. Fold in the coconut and lemongrass. Place in the refrigerator to chill for at least 30 minutes.

Cut the pineapple in thin, lengthwise pieces, creating "sheets" of pineapple.

Mix the mango and papaya together in a bowl.

Lay one-third of the pineapple sheets on a work surface

Spread a third of the whipping cream onto the pineapple.

Top with some mango and papaya. Follow this with another layer of pineapple, cream, and fruit.

Top with a final layer of pineapple, cream, and fruit.

Serve chilled and garnish with additional lemongrass, if desired.

Nutrition:

Calories: 128.5

Fat: 6.9 g

Carbs: 17.7 g

Protein: 1.0 g

Sugars: 6 g

Sodium: 80 mg

Ginger Peach Pie

Preparation Time: 10 minutes

Cooking Time: 45 minutes

Servings: 10

Ingredients:

5 c. diced peaches

½ c. sugar

2 refrigerated whole wheat pie crust doughs

1 tsp. cinnamon

½ c. orange juice

¼ c. chopped candied ginger

½ c. cornstarch

Directions:

Preheat the oven to 425°F.

Place one of the pie crusts in a standard size pie dish. Spread some coffee beans or dried beans in the bottom of the pie crust to use as a weight. Place the dish in the oven and bake for 10-15 minutes, or until lightly golden. Remove from the oven and let cool.

Combine the peaches, candied ginger, and cinnamon in a bowl. Toss to mix.

Combine the sugar, cornstarch, and orange juice in a saucepan and heat over medium until syrup begins to thicken.

Pour the syrup over the peaches and toss to coat.

Spread the peaches in the pie crust and top with the remaining crust. Crimp along the edges and cut several small slits in the top.

Place in the oven and bake for 25-30 minutes, or until golden brown.

Let set before slicing.

Nutrition:

Calories: 289.0

Fat: 13.1 g

Carbs: 41.6 g

Protein: 3.9 g

Sugars: 22 g

Sodium: 154 mg

Mocha Ricotta Cream

Preparation Time: 10 minutes

Cooking Time: 0 minutes

Servings: 4

Ingredients:

2 c. part skin ricotta cheese

1 tbsp. espresso powder

Almond cookie crumbs

½ c. powdered sugar

1 tbsp. dark cocoa powder

1 tsp. pure vanilla extract

Directions:

Combine the ricotta cheese, powdered sugar, espresso powder, cocoa powder, and vanilla extract in a bowl.

Using an electric mixer, blend until creamy.

Cover and refrigerate for at least 4 hours.

Serve in individual dishes, garnished with cookie crumbs, if desired.

Nutrition: Calories: 230.6 Fat: 9.9 g Carbs: 22.0 g Protein: 14.3 g Sugars: 3.2 g Sodium: 166 mg

Fresh Parfait

Preparation Time: 10 minutes

Cooking Time: 0 minutes

Servings: 6

Ingredients:

4 peeled and chopped grapefruits

2 tsps. grated lime zest

4 c. non-fat yogurt

2 tbsps. lime juice

1 tbsp. chopped mint

3 tbsps. stevia

Directions:

In a bowl, combine the yogurt using the stevia, lime juice, lime zest and mint and stir.

Divide the grapefruits into small cups, add the yogurt mix in each and serve.

Enjoy!

Nutrition: Calories: 200 Fat: 3 g Carbs: 15 g Protein: 10 g Sugars: 20 g Sodium: 13 mg

Toasted Almond Ambrosia

Preparation Time: 10 minutes

Cooking Time: 20 minutes

Servings: 2

Ingredients:

½ Cup Almonds, Slivered

½ Cup Coconut, Shredded & Unsweetened

3 Cups Pineapple, Cubed - 5 Oranges, Segment

1 Banana, Halved Lengthwise, Peeled & Sliced

2 Red Apples, Cored & Diced

2 Tablespoons Cream Sherry

Mint Leaves, Fresh to Garnish

Directions: Start by heating your oven to 325, and then get out a baking sheet. Roast your almonds for ten minutes, making sure they're spread out evenly. Transfer them to a plate and then toast your coconut on the same baking sheet. Toast for ten minutes. Mix your banana, sherry, oranges, apples and pineapple in a bowl. Divide the mixture not serving bowls and top with coconut and almonds. Garnish with mint before serving.

Nutrition: Calories: 177 Protein: 3.4 Grams Fat: 4.9 Grams Carbs: 36 Grams Sodium: 13 mg Cholesterol: 11 mg

Apple Dumplings

Preparation Time: 10 minutes

Cooking Time: 30 minutes

Servings: 4

Ingredients:

Dough:

1 Tablespoon Butter

1 Teaspoon Honey, Raw

1 Cup Whole Wheat Flour

2 Tablespoons Buckwheat Flour

2 Tablespoons Rolled Oats

2 Tablespoons Brandy or Apple Liquor

Filling:

2 Tablespoons Honey, Raw

1 Teaspoon Nutmeg

6 Tart Apples, Sliced Thin

1 Lemon, Zested

Directions:

Turn the oven to 350.

Get out a food processor and mix your butter, flours, honey and oats until it forms a crumbly mixture.

Add in your brandy or apple liquor, pulsing until it forms a dough.

Seal in a plastic and place it in the fridge for two hours.

Toss your apples in lemon zest, honey and nutmeg.

Roll your dough into a sheet that's a quarter inch thick. Cut out eight-inch circles, placing each circle into a muffin tray that's been greased.

Press the dough down and then stuff with the apple mixture. Fold the edges, and pinch them closed. Make sure that they're well sealed.

Bake for a half hour until golden brown, and serve drizzled in honey.

Nutrition:

Calories: 178

Protein: 5 Grams

Fat: 4 Grams

Carbs: 23 Grams

Sodium: 562 mg

Cholesterol: 61 mg

Apricot Biscotti

Preparation Time: 25 minutes

Cooking Time: 25 minutes

Servings: 4

Ingredients:

2 Tablespoons Honey, Dark

2 Tablespoons Olive Oil

½ Teaspoon Almond Extract

¼ Cup Almonds, Chopped Roughly

2/3 Cup Apricots, Dried

2 Tablespoons Milk, 1% & Low Fat

2 Eggs, Beaten Lightly

¾ Cup Whole Wheat Flour

¾ Cup All Purpose Flour

¼ Cup Brown Sugar, Packed Firm

1 Teaspoon Baking Powder

Directions:

Start by heating the oven to 350, and then mix your baking powder, brown sugar and flours in a bowl.

Whisk your canola oil, eggs, almond extract, honey and milk. Mix well until it forms a smooth dough. Fold in the apricots and almonds.

Put your dough on plastic wrap, and then roll it out to a twelve inch long and three inch wide rectangle. Place this dough on a baking sheet, and bake for twenty-five minutes. It should turn golden brown. Allow it to cool, and slice it to ½ inch thick slices, and then bake for another fifteen minutes. It should be crispy.

Nutrition:

Calories: 291

Protein: 2 Grams

Fat: 2 Grams

Carbs: 12 Grams

Sodium: 123 mg

Cholesterol: 21 mg

Apple & Berry Cobbler

Preparation Time: 10 minutes

Cooking Time: 30 minutes

Servings: 4

Ingredients:

Filling:

1 Cup Blueberries, Fresh

2 Cups Apples, Chopped

1 Cup Raspberries, Fresh

2 Tablespoons Brown Sugar

1 Teaspoon Lemon Zest

2 Teaspoon Lemon Juice, Fresh

½ Teaspoon Ground Cinnamon

1 ½ Tablespoons Corn Starch

Topping:

¾ Cup Whole Wheat Pastry Flour

1 ½ Tablespoons Brown Sugar

½ Teaspoon Vanilla Extract, Pure

¼ Cup Soy Milk

¼ Teaspoon Sea Salt, Fine

1 Egg White

Directions:

Turn your oven to 350, and get out six small ramekins. Grease them with cooking spray.

Mix your lemon juice, lemon zest, blueberries, sugar, cinnamon, raspberries and apples together in a bowl.

Stir in your cornstarch, mixing until it dissolves.

Beat your egg white in a different bowl, whisking it with sugar, vanilla, soy milk and pastry flour.

Divide your berry mixture between the ramekins and top with the vanilla topping.

Put your ramekins on a baking sheet, baking for thirty minutes. The top should be golden brown before serving.

Nutrition:

Calories: 131

Protein: 7.2 Grams

Fat: 1 Grams

Carbs: 13.8 Grams

Sodium: 14 mg Cholesterol: 2.1 mg

Conclusion

Now you know everything you need to in order to enjoy the benefits of the DASH diet. There's no reason to just deal with hypertension, but remember that even with his dietary change, you will still need any medication prescribed to your by your doctor as well as you'll need to exercise regularly to maintain your health and reap the full benefits. With regular exercise and healthy eating, a dietary approach to stopping hypertension is manageable. Don't let hypertension rule your life. Take back control by first taking back control of your diet.

www.ingramcontent.com/pod-product-compliance
Lightning Source LLC
Chambersburg PA
CBHW050349120526
44590CB00015B/1615